MANAGING
DEPRESSION
with QIGONG

of related interest

You Are How You Move
Experiential Chi Kung
Ged Sumner
ISBN: 978 1 84819 014 6

Yi Jin Jing
Tendon-Muscle Strengthening Qigong Exercises
The Chinese Health Qigong Association
ISBN: 978 1 84819 008 5

Ba Duan Jin
Eight-Section Qigong Exercises
The Chinese Health Qigong Association
ISBN: 978 1 84819 005 4

Liu Zi Jue
Six Sounds Approach to Qigong Breathing Exercises
The Chinese Health Qigong Association
ISBN: 978 1 84819 006 1

Wu Qin Xi
Five-Animal Qigong Exercises
The Chinese Health Qigong Association
ISBN: 978 1 84819 007 8

MANAGING
DEPRESSION
with QIGONG

Frances Gaik

SINGING DRAGON
London and Philadelphia

Figure 2.3 (Minegishi *et al.* 1998, p.43), Figures 3.1 and 3.2 (Kido 1997, p.66), Figure 3.3 (Shen, Tone and Lasayama 1999, p.95), and Figure 3.4 (Kawano 1998b, p.221) all reproduced by permission of the *Journal of International Society of Life Information Science.*

First published in 2009
by Singing Dragon
an imprint of Jessica Kingsley Publishers
116 Pentonville Road
London N1 9JB, UK
and
400 Market Street, Suite 400
Philadelphia, PA 19106, USA

www.singing-dragon.com

Library of Congress Cataloging in Publication Data
A CIP catalog record for this book is available from the Library of Congress

British Library Cataloguing in Publication Data
A CIP catalogue record for this book is available from the British Library

ISBN 978 1 84819 018 4

Printed and bound in the United States by
Thomson-Shore, 7300 W. Joy Road, Dexter, MI 48130

Contents

ACKNOWLEDGMENTS

I wish to thank Futoshi Yumoto for his work on the statistical analysis and compilation of the data from the research study. I also wish to thank the three qigong practitioners, Chunyi Lin, Renee Ryan and Jim Nance, who participated in the study, with special thanks to Chunyi Lin for allowing the Spring Forest Qigong Technique Guide to be included in this book. I would also like to give a special thank you to my husband, Casey, for his assistance with the preparation and organization of the research study sessions, his technical efforts in compiling the figures for the book as well as his continued support of my interests.

Introduction

If you or someone you know suffers from depression, this book offers more than hope; it offers a simple strategy for a way of moving from the darkness of despair to a more satisfied and healthy state of being. The material presented here may be used as part of a therapy treatment plan, or on your own, if you are not seeing a therapist. Change does not occur by accident, and it is more likely to occur with outside influence.

We change our behavior for any one of a number of reasons, but there are four in particular:

- because of monotony – we are tired of things the way they are

- because we are forced or compelled to change by some outside force

- because the pain is too great

- because it gives us gratification to change.

Change occurs over stages, even if you are not aware of it. Specifically, the *pre-contemplative stage*, when you don't even think there is a problem, it's just how things are; the *contemplative stage*, when you think there might be a problem, but don't know what to do about it; the *preparation stage*, when you are learning about the causes and what to do; the *action stage*, when you take action to correct the problem; and then *maintenance*, when you work to continue the new behavior which was helpful. You can apply these stages of change to behavior, thinking, your physical health, your interpersonal relationships, or even a habit or addiction.

If you are suffering from depression, or maybe you think you just might be sad and blue, this book will help to move you through these stages of change and provide you with a valuable new tool for overcoming the wall of depression which keeps you from living life to its fullest.

No matter how long you have suffered from depression, qigong can be an effective weapon in your battle. Perhaps you are depressed and you don't understand why or how this came to be. Perhaps you have tried several things, including medication and therapy, without much success; perhaps you have simply accepted that your situation will never get better. My research, presented here, indicates that qigong can provide a way to change the way you feel and how you look at the world. In a short period of time, if you practice qigong daily, you may well experience the benefits of the simple technique, and begin your road to recovery.

This book is presented as a self-help manual to describe the effectiveness of the Eastern technique of qigong (pronounced chee-gong) and how a simple daily practice can change your life. Qigong is an ancient form of active exercise done with meditation and intent. The movements are designed to aid your immune system and to adjust energy flow in the body. It will increase your energy and create a sense of health and peacefulness. It is based on traditional Chinese medicine and provides a holistic format to harmonize mind and body, boost your energy and improve your mood. I will discuss qigong at length and present my research findings in its application to depressive symptoms.

This book is based on my clinical research study, which took place in Oak Brook, Illinois, in the summer of 2002. The study, which lasted for two months, supported my findings that qigong can be an effective treatment for depression. I have written the material as if you were sitting in my office and we were talking about your problem and how to solve it, as I do with many of my own patients. I am going to walk you through the information and help you to make change happen. The research material provided serves as an educational component about qigong and is somewhat more detailed than the dissertation study publication (Gaik 2003). The book and the technique are not intended to replace any medication or therapy which you may be currently using; the practice is suggested as a supporting and complementary program to increase your health and well-being. I believe that you can improve your physical and mental health as a result of a daily practice of qigong. If you are feeling better and believe that your medication should be reviewed, you should consult with your doctor for a medical evaluation to adjust the medication slowly and with supervision.

I will present the strategy as it was applied in my clinical study, which utilized the Spring Forest Qigong technique as an alternative and complementary treatment for depression. The technique is made a part of this book and may be found in the Appendices.

The research study was immensely successful, and all subjects improved after using the technique of Spring Forest Qigong after a short time. The 39 participants in the final sample of the study were seriously depressed individuals, many of whom had lost hope about getting better. The group included three individuals who were suffering from bipolar disorder.

Qigong is not a secret; it has been around for more than five thousand years and practiced in the East by millions of people. Qigong exercise is more than just looking on the brighter side of things; it actively works to bring your body back into balance after the impact of your everyday life. I will present my research material and the science to support the evidence of my findings, and I will do so in a way that is readily understandable to you, with the strong recommendation that you begin a daily practice now. The practice is not exertive and, even if you are seriously ill, you can begin with lying-down exercises.

We will be looking at depression and the many ways it manifests to help you understand where the causes lie. Again, this is to assist you in the contemplation of the problem, as well as to prepare you for taking action to change. Today's world can be very stressful, and, indeed, there is a great deal to be anxious about. Depression can be driven by anxiety, and a feeling of your inability to change or control your situation. You feel stuck, overwhelmed, and your self esteem suffers. Depression has a chemical basis in your body and it affects your energy levels, perhaps to the point where you feel you can't do anything – let alone a daily exercise. Many of the people in my study felt this way, but had substantial gains after only a brief period of doing the qigong exercise. Even I was surprised by the degree of significant change in the people who participated. Sleep improved, they looked better, they had substantial gains in self esteem and energy, and they wanted to learn more about the qigong techniques.

I urge you to suspend your skepticism for a while, put down despair for just today, and begin a journey to getting better. Let's get ready for change.

Chapter 1

A Paradigm Shift toward Holistic Interventions

I shall assume that you don't know anything about qigong, and why it isn't practiced more widely in the West. Qigong is considered to be an energy treatment and there is currently a change going on in medical science with a more open attitude toward such treatments.

A paradigm shift occurs in the hard or instrumental sciences after researchers build a body of information leading toward a crisis, which is resolved by a dramatic shift in perspective (Kuhn 1970). Textbooks are then rewritten and the old paradigm all but disappears. Psychological research is modeled along the empirical hard sciences, as much as possible, in its effort to move toward greater acceptance as a relatively new science. The problem is, if we cannot measure it, it may be dismissed as insignificant or reduced to biochemical interactions (Larson, Wood and Larson 1993). No one has ever seen an atom, but we know it is there and how powerful it can be. It can be used for destruction, or it can be used as constructive energy, depending upon *intent.*

It is my belief that we are currently in the midst of such a paradigm crisis and shift, as some health care systems are failing to maintain an adequate level of care. The rising costs of technology and a demand for the highest level of care for all continue to spiral costs to a disproportionate level of the Gross National Product of all countries of the developed world. The current system is not always working and we know it. Consequently, some individuals have necessarily turned toward alternative methods to fill the gap. Our dependency upon science to resolve the problems of mastering the body and mind have created a vociferous monster that we can no longer afford to feed. The ultimate solution lies within the personal responsibility of the individual directed toward preventative care. The qigong technique in this book is a method for general health and can help you to maintain your health, both mental and physical.

Western medicine has the best technology and strategies for acute care. If you have a heart attack or you need surgery, you want to be in the best hospital and the best system for treating the problem. We naturally rely upon medicine to "fix" us when we are broken, and we tend to neglect the business of being healthy and well until an emergency necessitates medical treatment. However, we are not as good at preventative care as we should be. We have only begun to learn about the drastic effects of stress and negative emotions on the body with an eye toward living a more balanced life.

The symbol of the medical profession, the serpent on the staff of Asklepios, is meant to symbolize the body, mind and spirit, but it is a common belief that Western doctors attend to the physical aspects alone (Weil 1995). In the United States, doctors, forced by managed care restrictions and burdened by administrative costs, need to limit the time spent with patients so that more patients can be seen, in order to earn a decent living. Doctors may order tests as a normal procedure to limit their liability and their malpractice insurance costs. A successful medical practitioner can have a great bedside manner, but he or she also may need to be a good business person. This does not necessarily work toward the best interests of the patient.

If a neurologist, CAT (computed axial tomography) scan or EEG (electroencephalogram) cannot find a problem, it is determined to be psychosomatic and a referral is made to a psychologist. Mental health professionals, oriented to avoid spiritual issues unless the patient addresses them first, may create another void in the treatment process. I will show you how qigong addresses this void and can put you in touch with spirit, your healing source, and that it does so without addressing religious beliefs.

Eastern techniques strongly differ in their approach to addressing the needs of the individual. The Eastern concept of health is more inclined to consider the whole person, physical, mental and spiritual aspects combined. Holistic or integrative approaches to medicine which recognize the Eastern concept of the body's ability to strengthen internal defenses have been popularized and also highly criticized in the United States and other Western societies. In spite of the criticism, there is also a growing interest in alternative therapies which include bio-energy treatments. Patients are caught in the middle, wishing to have competent treatment utilizing the latest technology, yet their social, psychological and spiritual needs may be ignored. The vacuum has created a demand for the psychospiritual care by other than traditional sources and has opened the door to a host of charlatans and alternative medicine practitioners. Seven out of ten people who use alternative medicines do not discuss it with their doctors (Eisenberg *et al.* 1998), and what the established medical field does not understand may be labeled "new age" cultism or supernatural parapsychology (Levin and Coreil 1986).

Depression has been consistently researched in an effort to determine effective treatment and causes. Cultural expectations of an illusive state of "happiness" and well-being have created a significant demand for a rapid remedy. If you break up with your partner and you are having a difficult time, it is likely you will be prescribed medication by your general practitioner, and this may affect your motivation toward the overall insight into the problems of the relationship. The patient is satisfied to be numbed to the pain, remains functional, and it is cost-effective; or is it? Antidepressants have become a quick-fix in today's managed care environment. Pharmaceutical companies seeking a profitable return on their research investment are pressured to continue to refine their products and to promote distribution of the popular antidepressant drugs. This has resulted in an overwhelming reception by psychiatry and the general population. Wider use of antidepressants and other prescription drugs has reduced the role of psychotherapy (Mojtabai 2008), which limits patients' ability to resolve the underlying issues of their depression. Addressing the symptom does not solve the problem. Numbing the pain and getting back to our busy lives has other consequences in the long run and can likely manifest in other forms of illness.

The current "biopsychosocial model" predominates as the major paradigm in causal factors and treatment considerations for depression (Cronkite and Moos 1995; Thase and Glick 1995). There are many factors which may contribute to a state of depression and it is frequently found to exist along with both medical and psychological problems, creating a "dual" diagnosis. Depression can also range from a mild adjustment disorder as a response to an environmental challenge – what we may call a "situational depression" or an adjustment disorder – to symptoms of a full psychotic episode as outlined in the *Diagnostic and Statistical Manual* (DSM-IV) of the American Psychiatric Association (1994).

Generally, the most effective and common treatment for depression is cognitive behavioral therapy (CBT), which addresses the negative perception patterns of the events as experienced by the individual (Beck *et al.* 1979). Later we will be looking at cognitive perceptions and how they can trigger a flow of "negative" chemicals in the body. The supportive approach of interpersonal techniques has also been found to be successful in treatment settings (Depression Guideline Panel 1993). Interpersonal therapy focuses on providing support and hope to the patient. The therapist uses the personal relationship in the therapy setting to resolve the problems related to grief, interpersonal disputes or coping deficits.

If you suffer from serious depressive symptoms, the standard treatment protocol is currently to take a prescribed antidepressant medication and pair it with therapy. My research was the first attempt in a controlled clinical study to apply qigong as a treatment for depression, and the results indicate that qigong should be a regularly prescribed part of any treatment plan for depression to facilitate a more rapid and complete recovery.

Depression has a purpose in the realm of survival. Emotions are valuable tools for human interaction and growth. When you have an emotional injury, the sadness or depression you experience creates the need to pull away from the world and to "heal" the mind. This time will allow for a rebalance of the brain chemistry. If this occurs in an ideal, supportive, healthy environment, with acceptance that things will get better, your body begins the process of healing and your brain chemistry eventually stabilizes the system. This is where the insight of therapy or a personal confidant is helpful. If there is a continual or chronic situation which exacerbates the depression, or your biological chemistry is such that it is prone to depression, it can become more problematic. The association between what we perceive as uncontrollable events and depression is strong.

In marriages, when one partner suffers from depression, it can affect the marriage and couple therapy is advised. When the family is the source of the problem, the support structure is compromised and you need to seek couples or family counseling. Don't ignore the problem with the thought that it will go away. It will usually get bigger and compromise the health and balance of all members in the family unit. A mother or caretaker who suffers from depression may be unable to provide the emotional attachment necessary for the child; depression in a father can be expressed as disengagement, isolation or anger.

Qigong is meant to stabilize the internal system, but it is not a magic bullet that will solve your interpersonal problems. It is meant to help your mind-body system through the crisis when it occurs. It is preventative, in that it strengthens the immune system and your ability to cope. It cannot magically remove the issues which are creating the problems. It is a very powerful coping mechanism and tool to keep you strong and stable during the crisis.

In contrast to the Western need to master the biological body through science and technology, Eastern cultures have focused on transcendence of mental pain and suffering through a mastery of spiritual ascendancy of higher planes of consciousness. Suffering is ended by engagement of the forces that create it, much like the cognitive approach, but the focus is on the presence of the divine within as well as the connection to the cosmos (Judith 1996). Therapeutics of Chinese medicine rest upon five main principles: guidance toward Dao (The Way), diet, drugs, acupuncture and moxibustian (a technique used to influence the movement of qi or energy in the body's vessels). Sometimes massage and exercise may be added (Prioreschi 1995, p.153).

In Chinese medicine, emotions in the form of overactive passions are closely related to disease of the various organs of the body (Shen 1986), such as anger and the liver. Seyle (1956) has found that psychosomatic disease can be created by stress in the weakest part of the body, and it will break down if the conditions persist. Alfred Adler, a psychologist, saw the same effects in the people he treated. Adler was one of the "big three" – Freud, Jung and Adler. Adler took a more practical approach with his patients, working with the population in a tailor district of his time.

Adlerian psychology is based on a holistic view of the individual, and Adler believed that "organ inferiority" or other inherent tendency created a need of overcompensation to feel adequate (Adler 1907). Adler is also known for the concept of the "inferiority complex." This is manifested in many ways in the personality and the body. He saw that many psychological issues manifested in similar physical problems, or that certain mental health issues related to a specific organ.

Adler wrote that "some day it will be proved that every organ inferiority may respond to psychological influences and speak the organ language, that is, a language expressing the attitude of the individual towards the problems confronting him" (Ansbacher and Ansbacher 1956, p.308). This "organ jargon" (pp.222–225) can be correlated with different psychological difficulties, but while Adler may have experienced this in his practice, he was not the first to recognize such patterns. This is something we see in ancient Eastern psychology and the study of qigong.

Theoretically, in traditional Chinese medicine, blockages at certain energy centers or meridian points can manifest into illness. As an Adlerian-trained therapist, interested in testing the hypothesis for myself, I have also found that there is usually a corresponding emotional block to a certain illness or medical condition. Adler was also a proponent of being connected with the outside world as a basis for a good support structure and good mental health, something which he called social interest. As our world continues to grow smaller, Adler's concept of social interest as a standard of wellness and adjustment is an idea whose time has come. This concept is closely related to the ancient Eastern concepts of social adjustment.

Social interest is the state of being connected with the world – something which the depressed person is not. When you are depressed, you likely withdraw and become isolated. This behavior cuts you off from your family and loved ones and further amplifies the problem as you begin to brood, thinking that no one understands your situation or problems. The depressed person wants to hide his or her head under the bed covers on the worst of days. In the Spring Forest Qigong practice, one of the movements is to reach up and out over your head to derive energy from the universe. They are diametrically opposed positions and states of mind.

Energy medicine is more and more frequently being used in the treatment of chronic illness. We think of it as new, but it is actually thousands of years old, derived from ancient cultures. The Western acculturation of energy treatments has taken the form of massage, body psychotherapies which include bioenergetics, biodynamic psychotherapy and Chiron holistic psychotherapy. Emotional massage includes Rolfing, postural integration and biodynamic massage (Westland 1993). Shiatsu, Reiki, polarity therapy, acupuncture, acupressure, yoga, Reichian body work, holotropic integration and tai chi are other forms of energy work adopted in the West (Harris 1994).

Brent Baum's work with trauma victims using his technique of Holographic Memory Resolution is another form of energy work which is geared to assist in mastering states of consciousness (Baum 1997). Baum's technique utilizes the hand to scan the energy body for trauma, which is felt in the hands of the practitioner. He projects energy through the body at the neck vertebra Cervical 7 to further facilitate the traumatic memory and its resolution. Likewise, qigong practitioners also scan the body's energy field with their hands and also work with Cervical 7, where an opening exists in the spinal column.

Energy psychology techniques are rooted in physics and challenge current psychological theories such as behavioral and cognitive methods (Gallo 2002). The different energy techniques are numerous and may incorporate tapping at or applying pressure to meridian points, utilizing an affirmation, or moving the eyes to create a balance in the energy field. These various energy techniques which intervene in the vibrational or electromagnetic field can bring a deep relaxation and reduction in muscle tension and pain. They can accelerate wound healing and are very useful in pre- and post-operation situations. Interestingly, the patient does not need to believe in the process, but needs only to be receptive to experience a benefit.

A mind-body intervention which creates the relaxation response (RR) will affect physical aspects in the body. They need not be Eastern or esoteric techniques, but they should be something you enjoy doing to insure that you will maintain the practice. Repetitive prayer, meditation, breathing exercises, progressive relaxation, biofeedback, guided imagery and hypnosis are all known to be useful in pain management and inhibiting the stress response.

Herbert Benson first described the relaxation response in the mid-1970s and his team's most recent findings are compelling evidence that it is possible to change your genetic destiny (Benson 1975; Dusek et al. 2008).

This exciting research has shown that the relaxation response which occurs during qigong and these other techniques can actually influence the expression of stress-related genes (Dusek et al. 2008). The relaxation response will affect heart rate, blood pressure, oxygen consumption and brain activity. The Benson team's clinical study is at the cutting edge of efforts to intervene in the genetic aspects of complex disorders which we have previously believed are simply a matter of our biology.

In this research, certain specific genes which are affected by processes such as inflammation or which are likely to be damaged by illness were measured with sensitive analyses. *In both short- and long-term practices of techniques which elicit the relaxation response – such as qigong – there were changes in how the gene responded.* The results suggest that consistent and constitutive changes in those genes may relate to long-term physiological effects and alter the expression of those genes. This study shows that your mental state can affect your genetic make-up. It further confirms that you are not a victim of your genes and your biology. Qigong, by activating the relaxation response, may actually switch off the patterns of stress gene activity which affect your body and your mind. The mind-body is one, and qigong can be a very effective intervention in turning things around quickly, as my own research indicates.

This new paradigm for understanding disease and physical ailments as they correlate with emotion is emerging and it addresses the subtle energies and blockages within the body, the electromagnetic field and the new discoveries of quantum physics (Davidson 1987; Myss 1996; Page 2000; Zohar 1990). Some of the mind-body research points toward the repression of emotion as it relates to certain diseases, such as hopelessness and cancer (Wood 1985). As we learn more about DNA, the human genome and the impact of emotions on health, science is beginning to give energy treatments a second look.

The trend toward integrative medicine and a holistic focus on the mind-body-spirit requires a multidimensional approach. There is little doubt that these energy-related treatments are making a difference in how people respond and heal. One of the participants in my study commented "There is definitely something there" when first beginning to practice the technique.

You can feel this "something" for yourself. Sit quietly for a moment and concentrate on your breath. Center yourself; pull your focus into your body. Close your eyes and take several deep and slow breaths. Now extend your arms with bent elbows directly in front of you. Lightly open your fingers and slowly move your hands, palms facing, toward each other, as if you were going to hold a ball. Slowly, move the hands closer to each other until you feel something between the hands. You won't need to touch the hands, as you will feel it before you touch. Some people feel it as a spongy mass, and some will feel a tingling at the finger tips. This is your energy field. It extends all around your body and is especially sensitive to your hands where there are many nerve endings. Make its acquaintance, because this is where we are going to focus our work with qigong. You can also practice by feeling the energy of another person to become more sensitive to it.

Maintaining good mental health is more than popping a pill. It can only be achieved by taking personal responsibility for your health and the achievement of a sense of peace, well-being and acceptance. Claim your vitality and take your life back. The daily practice of qigong can be a good place to start.

· Chapter 2 ·

The Information System
of Your Body

Chunyi Lin, who developed the Spring Forest Qigong technique, speaks about the body getting "bad information" which creates blockages and illness. In this chapter, we are going to be looking at how this bad information is derived, how a blockage may occur and how you can change it with qigong and some other cognitive techniques. Understanding the system and its function is the key to change and this chapter should be considered to be a manual to your mind-body.

Let's take a look at how your body makes energy and transfers information. Your body is made up of cells; some are different than others. You have blood cells and muscle cells and the neurons have electrical properties which "fire" and transfer information. The neurons are where most of the action exists. Every cell has a nucleus which contains genetic material known as DNA. The exceptions are those which have chromosomes, the sperm and the egg. Genes are nothing more than long segments of DNA – the building blocks of who you are. The twisting of the DNA helix gives it strength and structure. The DNA provides the "address" for many functions of the system and, as you are aware, contains your genetic inherited ancestry.

Put simply, the communication process of cells occurs through a complex transcription and a translation of instructions with proteins and amino acids. The cells have a body or soma, as well as axons and dendrites which extend out to reach to other cells. You may recall this from your old biology class. The axons are the output device or how a neuron communicates with other neurons. You may remember that they don't actually touch – but that there is a space or synapse between the axon and the dendrite or the "antenna" of the next neuron (Figure 2.1). This synapse and the chemicals in the space between are most important toward good mental health.

The cell body contains mitochondria, which is where the cells take in nutrients and turn it into usable energy. Remarkably, the mitochondria can take in one unit of "input" and create seventeen units of usable energy or ATP (adenosine triphosphate). ATP is the energy currency that fuels biochemical reactions in neurons; it is required for cellular activity.

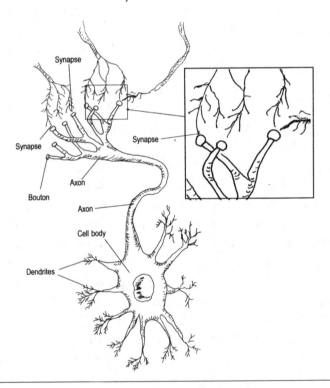

Figure 2.1 A neuron showing the cell body and axon connection with the dendrites; the inset illustration highlights the boutons at the synapse transmission site

There are changes in ATP levels when qigong is practiced and when the "qigong state" is entered. Blood levels of ATP increase significantly, indicating a storing of energy. When qigong masters transfer energy, or emit qi, their ATP levels drop considerably (Wang, Huang and Wu 1988). These physiological changes which occur in the physical body don't necessarily give us any clear indication of the nature of qi or how qi makes the change occur. But we can surmise that internal processes are benefiting through a stronger and more energized system.

The purpose of a neuron is information transfer, and it is accomplished effectively and efficiently when the healthy system is running well. A system of interconnecting neurons sends information coursing down through the neurons with an electrical and chemical process. Each neuron gets input from thousands of other neurons and it happens extremely quickly, within milliseconds of time elapse. One single charge can release a "cascade" to thousands of other neurons. This provides you with the ability of necessary action in movement, especially in an emergency. The communication between your brain and your body are constant, even in sleep, when the subconscious is active in processing the day. The chemicals which formulate the process are called neurotransmitters, and they play a critical role in psychological health as well. Unfortunately, negative thoughts can cascade the same way and affect the body quickly and immediately. This process is the information highway of all human functioning.

In depressive disorders the neurotransmitter of serotonin (5H-T) is a key component. Antidepressants are commonly known as SSRIs (selective serotonin reuptake inhibitors). They work by interfering with the normal chemical synaptic transmission. SSRIs such as Prozac, Zoloft and Paxil block the reuptake of the serotonin, which is at the synapse or space between the two communicating cells. This allows the serotonin to remain floating in the space between the sending and receiving cell for a longer period of time (Figure 2.2).

In order for any neurotransmitter to transfer, it must fit or bind into a special receptor just like a key which fits only a certain lock.

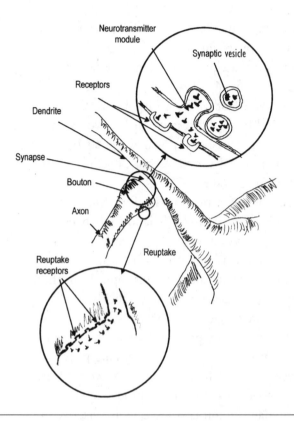

Figure 2.2 One of the many synaptic junctures of the neuron; the top inset illustration shows how the neurotransmitter enters the receptor sites in vesicles, while the bottom inset indicates the reuptake point on the transmitting axon

When the receptor opens, if the neurotransmitter "fits" with the receptor, it transmits, the receptor closes and then opens again. Any leftover serotonin stays in the synapse or space between the two cells for a time and then it is taken back up into the initiating sending unit to be broken down and recycled in the body's efficient process. By blocking the reuptake we allow the serotonin to be more accessible for another available chance at transmission. If the serotonin is allowed to float longer, there is a better chance of transmission when the receptor on the receiving cell is free or open again. It has greater opportunity to bind into that special keyhole. The SSRI blocks the reuptake of the serotonin by "gunking" up the return site where it would be recycled. It has a similar "key" structure, but not quite exact. This is what creates side effects from the medication. The less exact the key structure, the greater incidence of side effects. There are numerous forms of antidepressants, but this is the essential action of the SSRI mechanism.

The antidepressant action of the medication takes several weeks to develop completely, even though there are immediate effects on the transmission at the modulating synapses. If you go off the drug, it should be done slowly, under the guidance of your physician. This is because the body may adjust to the medication and make less serotonin because it isn't needed. Your body thinks it has enough because more of it has been "hanging out" between the cells and your body tends to be efficient, so it will not make what it doesn't need. Your system needs to adapt over time.

Let's think about the brain and the neuron system as the "hardware" of the information processing system similar to that of a computer. It runs the system automatically and efficiently. Humans are not computers, however; they are individual and unique and they have free will; they take action with intent. When information is processed by humans, it requires attention, perception, thought processes and decision before action. This is all accomplished through the neural system and this is known as cognition. Using the metaphor of the computer, we might think of cognition as the "software" of the system.

It is important to understand the cognitive system in order to help you to create the potential for change in your feelings of depression. Knowledge is power and, if you understand how negative thinking works against your information system, you will have a better chance of making change occur.

If we think about the software as a program for the computer, we want to have a really great software "package" to operate the system as efficiently as possible. The way you perceive the world directly affects your emotions or what we call your affect. The pattern of the associations and type of meaning people put on things gives us our understanding of what is called "schema." The world is filtered through your schema, or your belief system, and everyone has their own individual schema or software program. If you are prone to listening to others who are disapproving or critical, the program of others can become your "mirror" and you will feel badly about yourself. The more you feel badly about yourself, your self esteem suffers and you feel inadequate to try new things, ultimately affecting your confidence and well-being.

This helps us to understand complex disorders such as depression. Today, we understand that depression can be thought of in terms of a vicious circle of cognitive processing in which the mistaken beliefs or biased appraisals of the person lead to feeling more depressed. The depression biases the appraisals even further in the negative direction. This can be likened to the computer language terminology "garbage in – garbage out."

So it is really important to examine your thinking and the source of your appraisals. Rational decisions which we make are not necessarily based on logic, they are made on what you might think is reasonable, even in spite of the conflicting evidence. This is commonly called "cognitive dissonance." Your brain is actually wired for self justification to condone any misbehavior. Because we are aware of a gap between our self image and our actual behavior, we minimize the dissonance by justifying what we do to preserve our good opinion of ourselves. We might persuade ourselves that we are acting in the right way when, in fact, it may not be beneficial. This is the job of the ego, which utilizes a number of defense mechanisms, some good and some which can create difficulty. In depressed individuals, the ego strength may be lacking and they blame themselves as a negative pattern. Building on your strengths and increasing your positive appraisal of yourself will help you to become more confident and it will build ego strength.

Healthy defense mechanisms are really important to our mental functioning. For instance, we might repress the feeling that we aren't very confident about making a formal presentation in order to get through the ordeal successfully. That is beneficial. If we have denial about the need to be prepared for the presentation because of laziness or arrogance, or think that the "cards" are stacked against us, that can create difficulty. Both repression and denial are defense mechanisms, but the ability to repress is a higher-level defense function. Denial and repression are both similar and different in their nature, and both have very different results. Exercise courage and move to stretch outside your comfort zone, even if you won't do it perfectly.

The software program you built

So how does this schema or system develop? When you were a child, you had to figure out a lot of things about your surroundings. You had to learn to "fit in" with your first social system – the family. You learned the expectations and the values and assimilated many of those into your own thinking. Then later, in school, you encountered a bigger social setting. As creative as you are, you pick up cues from your parents, your siblings, the environment, and other people's actions in learning how to be in the world. You develop the programs in your brain as part of the socialization process. Perhaps as you got older, you discarded some of the things you learned from parents and your culture because it didn't fit with what you experienced in the world.

Socialization is a very powerful behavior modifier which causes us to comply with the norms of our group. This learning is rapid and enhances the mental information processes for the efficient use of that knowledge. No need to continually figure something out, it becomes "labeled" with some immediate understanding. Some examples might be "Fire is hot, don't touch," or "If I misbehave, I am harshly punished," or "I need to be perfect." Many factors influence the belief system such as the environment, parents, siblings, birth order – but it is the interpretation of these which forms the schema, or the filter. If you are born blind, you have the ability to become a Helen Keller or you can feel slighted and impaired. This is the gift of free will and spirit.

The brain is efficient and "hardwires" its systems for economy and ease of processing. It hardwires something by making strong connections in the neurons which transmit the information. The hardwiring is more likely if a stronger emotion is connected to the experience. That's both a benefit and a liability. It's a great benefit to learning and survival, but if we encounter something that doesn't make sense in our belief system, we may tend to ignore it or "filter" it out. There's a great film called *What the Bleep Do We Know!?* that demonstrates this filtering action of the brain which I often recommend to my patients for a quick understanding of how this works. The book version is also available by Arntz, Chasse and Vincente (2005).

Evaluating your mistaken beliefs or cognitive distortions

Using an Adlerian technique of evaluating early recollections, we can appreciate how easily the brain "wires" itself with mistaken goals or interfering ideas. Let's try something with your own belief system. Pick an early recollection – anything – as long as it is something you remember under the age of 10 years. Remember it in as much detail as you can and perhaps write it out. It will be easy to recall the most vivid part of the memory, so make a note of that; and now remember what the feeling is connected to the memory. If you can write out about three or four of them, it's a good start to see your filter in action. It should not be a memory like "We always went to the lake…" It needs to be a single event, such as "This one time we went to the lake…" When you are done, let's look at how to interpret them. In a formal evaluation, I use eight of these and can readily pick up a pattern which points to a self-perpetuating loop in the presenting problem.

Look at each recollection and give it a "headline" as if it were a headline for a story for the newspaper. You will see a theme that pops out, and then look at the underlying belief. Sometimes it can be obvious, and other times it is just beneath the surface. Here's an example:

Memory: I was riding my bike for the first time without training wheels and my father was running behind me and pushing me. He was yelling, "Go, go, go!" Then he let go and I was racing along without anyone holding me. I was going faster and smiling. My older brother jumped in the way, I had to turn quickly and then I fell, scraping my arm. I was crying and hurt.

Vivid: The crash and feeling the scrape of my arm on the sidewalk.

Feeling: Angry and scared.

The theme or headline could be "Success Sabotaged" or it could be "Failed First Attempt." There are a lot of beliefs that pop out:

- "Men [father] help me to maintain my balance; therefore I need assistance."

- "Men [brother] get in my way and disrupt my efforts; therefore I am a victim."

- "I am unable to maintain my balance without assistance; therefore I am dependent on others."

- "Men cheer me on and push me to excel; therefore I need reassurance and support."

- "I get hurt when I try new things; therefore I won't, I'll play it safe."

- It can even extend to "I'm a failure" if we have enough of these which pop up.

The key to the interpretation is the most vivid part, which is what got encoded or hardwired because it was more emotional, and hence becomes part of the schema. The memory above is about the crash and the injury, not the success. The feeling is being angry and scared, in spite of the fact that there was smiling and obvious pride about an accomplishment. That is where the "guiding line" of the schema or perception interferes with the belief system. That is the problematic schema that filters the facts, and if we had more memories, it would likely be exhibited in those as well. The work of therapy is to reframe the thinking to see the accomplishment – and this will actually rewire the system.

The memory is stored in the subconscious, but it is part of the information data bank. So when this person is moving along successfully in life and someone appears to be getting in the way, the subconscious memory of the brother getting in the way will be tapped by the neural system, the emotions of anger and fear will arise, and the defense mechanism goes into action. They might respond with anger, or pull back in fear to retreat and brood. If they brood long enough and isolate as part of a pattern, seeing things as unfair, depression could set in.

The greater awareness you have about yourself, the more insight you develop about who you are, the greater your ability to remain on solid ground when an adverse situation presents itself. Things happen to all of us in life; it is inevitable that some problems will arise. *It is not what happens, but how we interpret and respond, that makes the difference.* Maintaining a solid sense of self and awareness is the key to personal growth and satisfaction, and qigong is an excellent tool which can help you to maintain balance and the solid sense of self.

The schema of our everyday consciousness has developed a neural system which filters and interprets experience. It makes you, you. It makes your personality what it is. The neural system is directly connected to every avenue of motor and chemical response available to the brain and it monitors body states and connects the brain with all physical functioning and sensory input. This neural pattern can be made conscious and manifest in a feeling, or it could be activated, but not necessarily be expressed. This is a covert response, or one which may be termed subconscious. This is important because it can bias the cognitive processes and influence the reasoning and decision-making mode without awareness. Sights, smells, sounds, songs can trigger a host of memories associated with an emotional event. And I want you to remember that the body's response is to trigger the cascade of neurotransmitters regardless of whether it is a good or bad memory. If you are continually tapping into negative memories, this will result in depressive thoughts and bad information by way of the neurotransmitters. Your body is reliving the memory on a chemical basis again and again.

In the early recollection example we just processed, the belief system could limit the effort of the individual, ideas about success, stability, as well as partner-relational issues. Early recollections relating to gender are usually how we frame our ideas about what a spouse should be and our own role in a relationship. Part of the real work in relationship counseling is to get each individual to see how they are contributing to the synergy of the dysfunctional pattern. If you are interested in doing additional work on your own belief system or need help with interpreting your early recollections, please visit my website (www.lifecoachdoc.net), which lists the services I provide. Any work you do on understanding the interfering belief systems is basic to understanding the negative patterns which create problems such as depression or anxiety.

The neural response patterns of your mind-body, the schema, is the software package constructed by you in your efforts at socialization or fitting in, while taking cues from your environment. It is the program you designed and it is running on autopilot. The first step is awareness of what the program is about. Changing the pattern is possible, especially with the help of a therapist, but new response mechanisms and learning take time and effort and qigong can help you to accomplish this more rapidly. It is necessary to move the energy in the body and open channels which have been blocked. This is the primary mechanism of the qigong exercise.

The active participation of the mind-body does not discriminate between a true statement and a false statement, because all thoughts are equal in biochemistry. You know this when you are frightened by something, and then realize it was nothing to be concerned about. Cognition is a process to which the emotional experience is integral and necessary. It is the initiating thought which gets most people into trouble or which sparks the creative genius. Mind is the builder and the world as we perceive it is largely a product of our evolving consciousness. I hope that you will continue to grow and learn with each new experience and keep your mind open and aware to how your belief systems limit the accuracy of your data input.

Some common limitations to your thinking can be the following:

- You magnify the negative aspects of things while filtering out the positive.

- You think in black and white; it's either all good or all bad.

- You blame others for your situation or your pain, or blame yourself for problems.

- You generalize outcomes; if something bad happens you expect it to happen again.

- You catastrophize and expect disaster; this is "what if" to the extreme.

- You personalize events; it's not necessarily about you.

- You feel like a victim because you feel others are in control.

- You need to be right and continually try to prove it.

- You feel resentful because things are not fair.

- You expect all your sacrifices to pay off.

- You keep score and are bitter when you are not treated with reciprocal behavior.

Organic considerations

If you had a difficult childhood and it was particularly discouraging, if you have a family history of depression, or if you have been diagnosed with clinical depression, the hardwiring can be especially problematic because the negative experience has been prolonged and more severe. Researchers have produced direct evidence that people prone to depression – even when they are feeling well – have abnormal mood-regulating brain circuitry. This makes them vulnerable to relapse when the levels of certain brain chemical messengers fall. The trait abnormality is in the systems utilizing the neurochemicals of dopamine and norepinephrine. Decreased dopamine, in particular, can trigger an increase in runaway activity of emotion centers deep in the brain. This is experienced as a loss of ability to experience pleasure (Fromm *et al.* 2008). Dopamine is closely associated with the pleasure receptors in the brain, and the inability to experience pleasure is a serious condition known as anhedonia. This is different than not enjoying yourself for the evening; it is a condition which is commonly found in clinical depression and serious mental disorders.

Neurochemicals are the information messengers of the system, as we have seen earlier. Candace Pert, who discovered the dopamine receptor, writes about the biological effects of negativity on the body in *Molecules of Emotion* (Pert 1999). The book is an interesting and inspiring chronicle of her discovery as well as her professional trials and efforts in a male-dominated field and is good recommended reading. She details how the "neuropeptides" (the neurotransmitters) determine the emotional oscillations in mood and emotion. The information system and network pathways get blocked and may be in a disrupted feedback loop to expect negative outcomes, which becomes a self-fulfilling prophecy. A suppression of "good information" occurs and the receptors for them shrink in size and decrease in number. The depression progresses to the point where it is having an impact at a cellular level. In severe cases, we might even see a shrinking in the hypothalamus, a small but an important part of the brain which regulates changing emotional states of the human organism.

When you shut down on your feelings and get into this negative feedback loop, you stop the flow of the feel-good neurotransmitters (dopamine) and the healing process. This is why you might feel stuck, but this can be reversed. The qigong exercise can help to stimulate the natural release of serotonin and dopamine, the good information, and to open blockage of the information system. Pert (1999, p.276) hypothesizes that the subtle energy of qi is actually "the free flow of information carried by the biochemicals of emotion, the neuropeptides of their receptors."

The free flow of information may be one of the effects of qigong, but as yet no one can truly say what the nature of the mysterious qi is for sure. I believe it is more than just the free flow of information, because it can be transferred from one person to another and the effects are readily observed and can be measured. We will have more about this in Chapter 3.

Energy-changing strategies combined with cognitive restructuring

My research indicated that qi can be measured in different formats which further sparked my interest in initiating my study with qigong and depression. As we have seen, serotonin (5-HT) and dopamine (DA) are key players in the depression pathology. Qigong can affect these neurotransmitters directly. Minegishi *et al.* (1998) found that there were significant increases in blood serotonin and B-endorphin concentration in trained subjects after a 30-minute qigong exercise period in comparison with an untrained control group. The levels were maintained even after a 30-minute rest, reflecting a calm and peaceful state (Figure 2.3).

In another study, a variation of the neurotransmitters such as 5-hydroxytamine (5-HT), norepinephrine (NE) and dopamine (DA) were monitored before and after qigong exercises. A comparison of pre- and post-exercise showed a general reduction in 5-HT, and NE and DA tended to go up. The post-exercise blood content of dopamine in the various groups rose remarkably (Liu *et al.* 1988; Liu, Jiao and Li 1990).

If we can reverse the blockage in the neural pathways by using qigong, we open the channels and pathways of the information system. We experience it as energy, because the body chemistry is allowed to do what it is meant to do. The research indicates that qigong can increase levels of serotonin and dopamine in the body without the interference of the reuptake process as seen with anti-depressant medication. The natural process and systems of the body

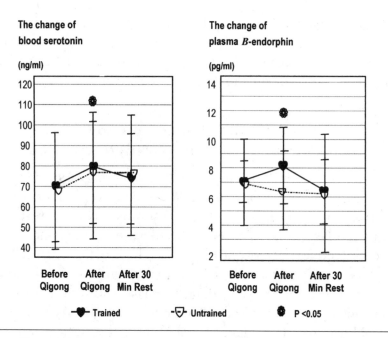

The change of blood serotonin (ng/ml)

The change of plasma *B*-endorphin (pg/ml)

Before Qigong   After Qigong   After 30 Min Rest

Before Qigong   After Qigong   After 30 Min Rest

Trained   Untrained   P <0.05

Figure 2.3 After doing qigong, participants experienced a significant level of increase in their serotonin levels; they maintained an increased level even after a 30-minute cessation of the exercise

are not interfered with, and the practitioner has a feeling of calm and peacefulness.

The plasticity of the brain is well known. If individuals have experienced a stroke or some injury, it may be difficult to learn to use their left hand for writing, if they normally use their right hand. It is possible, however, with continued effort and patience. The brain rewires the neural connections and a new behavior is possible. If you apply this same principle to your thinking, you will change the behavior of the information system. If the qigong practice is continued and an effort is made to change the thinking, or the cognition, the information system will improve by the type of information or neurotransmitter that is released. It is possible to retrain your mind and to minimize the destructive emotions and depression which seems to be overwhelming at this time. Many people, once they recognize the problematic thinking, complain about how hard it is to change the automatic response. It is hard, at first. But with patience and practice, and by using qigong to facilitate the flow, it becomes second nature and then suddenly, one day, you realize that you used to think differently before.

Techniques for change: moving from contemplation and preparation to action

Changing your thinking begins with monitoring your thoughts and reactions to events in your life. We need to increase your awareness for the destructive thought processes. You can begin with the early recollection exercise (see p.30) and make a list of some of the interfering ideas you might have. Next, look at the common list of limitations which might be part of your regular patterns. These are the triggers for negative thinking. Make a list of the negative thinking patterns which you feel need to be changed, and what you would like them to be. For example: "I never get the appreciation I deserve" can be changed to "Although my efforts may go unnoticed at times, I am loved for who I am." Then set a goal, such as "I will learn to respect my own boundaries and say 'no' when I am overburdened."

Now, set your *intent* to make a change in your thinking and your behavior. If you are a spiritual person, you might ask for divine assistance and help in your effort. If you are not particularly spiritual, you might call upon the universe for aid. By doing so, you invite the energy connected with the intent into your personal life. This is an important aspect of the action facet of the change model.

With increased awareness, you will be able to catch yourself when you are in these negative responses. Catching it can be made into a game with yourself. You will first feel it in your body. When you are getting tense or uptight about something or someone, pay attention to where you feel it in your body. I, personally, will usually set my jaw or my shoulders will tense. When I feel that, I know I need to relax or back off a bit. Everyone is different, so you need to monitor your own body. Maybe you feel a sinking feeling in your chest area, as if a weight were placed upon it – a particularly common feeling with those who are depressed.

By the time the body reaction appears, the thought is processed and the neurotransmitters have cascaded down for the insult upon the system. I liken it to "toxic waste" in the pipeline. The odd thing about it is you are the one who is polluting the system and it could be with subtle covert thoughts in the background. To free yourself from the control of these thoughts, practice these few steps and some of the following suggestions below. It will be cumbersome at first, but don't forget, you are rewiring the system, changing a lifetime of mental habits. It will get easier with continued effort of the strategy below, and also by doing the qigong practice.

Thought stopping

When you catch yourself in the negative thought, close your eyes for just a moment and visualize a big red stop sign. Breathe deeply. Breathe directly "into" the area where you feel the tension. Continue to breathe into the area until you feel it relax. Embrace yourself with a kind approach, without criticism. Then replace the negative thought with a more constructive and positive one. Visualize the healing energy of qi (you can use the visualization of light) moving through the system to the spot in your body where you felt tense and take a deep breath. The light is coming in from every pore of your body. Continue to breathe "into" the area. When you are done, remember to express gratitude for the healing.

If you feel that you are approaching a difficult, tension-filled zone, visualize a railroad crossing gate coming down. You will need to wait and exercise caution. Use this visualization to put a space between the event and your immediate reaction. Nobody likes to wait for a train; we want to be on our way. This exercise, however, can give you the time and space to change a negative reaction into a positive response. It becomes a form of "witnessing" or developing the "observing ego" (strengthening the ego) which can then safely modulate your behavior. It is enhanced greatly by meditation. This can be a simple five-minute meditation of simply "watching" your breath. You sit with eyes closed and focus on your breath as it comes in and out of your body at your nose, or you can focus on the rise and fall of your chest or stomach. Sit quietly and focus. If your mind wanders, come back to the breath. Eventually you will get good at it and you can extend the time, if you like.

If you are in a conflict with someone, remove yourself for a moment. You can easily say, "Excuse me," and take a few minutes to collect yourself. If you are alone and brooding on your life situation, use the stop sign to break the pattern and get up and do something else for a while, but don't forget to use the breathing to clear the area. If you can't leave a meeting, you can visualize a white shield of light in front of you, protecting you from the negative encounter. You can also visualize changing the channel on the radio or television. You are changing to a higher frequency, one which doesn't pick up the negative static. If you are feeling particularly generous, you might envision the white light around the source of the negativity in an act of compassion. Encase yourself in your own bubble of white light, without the two of you touching bubbles. Realize that this "attack" is part of the individual's own personal mistaken belief system. It isn't really about you; it is about their need to relate their own "story."

Boundaries and forgiveness

If you are unable to find compassion for someone who is in conflict with you, it would be most beneficial to work on forgiveness and good boundaries. Realize that the anger and hatred that you may hold for someone is affecting the body chemistry and creating bad information which only hurts you. You need not condone or approve of the person's conduct, letting them off the hook, so to speak. You do need to forgive them and release the energy that you devote toward the anger and hatred which spews the toxic waste into your system. You forgive them for *your* benefit, not for their benefit.

Practicing good boundaries can alleviate a great deal of pain and conflict in your life. Recognize your physical and emotional limitations. If you are feeling particularly resentful to someone, perhaps you have overextended yourself more than you should. This might be your boss, your spouse, your children, or just the world in general. Learn to say "no" and respect your own needs. The stress of attempting to please others can be a big factor in your illness. An overloaded system is pumping adrenalin and cortisol into the body and creating a false sense of emergency. This is particularly toxic because, if it is a consistent lifestyle, your energy will be depleted. If you are depressed because you have taken on too much, you need to evaluate your reasonable capabilities and make adjustments. If you are the victim of an abusive past, realize that you are only hurting yourself by hanging on to and replaying the memories. Get the help of a therapist to help you move out of the victim role and into the survivor mode. Energy therapists who practice techniques to release such trauma are especially recommended.

Visualization

I do a good deal of work with hypnosis and visualization techniques with athletes, which can enhance sport performance. If you are able to use visualization of a changed behavior in particularly troublesome situations, you will actually be modifying your physical neural connections by using your imagination. Practicing a response in your mind is a proven method to rewire the brain.

The visualization of the light energy bubbles is very effective in creating a safe environment for a short period of time. When you use the technique, you will likely notice a change in the attitude of the person confronting you. Your intent has changed and you are no longer open to the negativity. If you put a shield up, you can visualize the negativity bouncing off. One woman I worked with visualized this as colored sparks, as if it were a welder's torch by-product. It helped her to not become engaged in arguments with her husband when he was obstinate. If you can interrupt the usual synergy, the dynamic will change. Similar to the "stop sign" approach, we are attempting to put a space between thought and action, or reaction, as the case may be. Step outside the conflict with your observing ego. It takes only one person to change the dynamic.

A very effective energy technique can be used to clear your energy field in the shower every morning. After cleansing your body, stand in the shower and put one hand up to touch the metal shower head and place one or both feet on the metal drain. Now visualize the water washing away all the negativity from your body's energy field and see it going down the drain. Use the affirmation, "I cleanse my body, I cleanse my mind, I cleanse my spirit." You can repeat it several times. You will notice a difference in how you feel, especially over time.

Here is another technique. Lie down and relax in a quiet spot and visualize tension and stress moving down your body, beginning at the top of the head. Feel it as warmth, moving downward. See the stress and tension melting away, just as if it were butter melting in a pan; the edges getting round and soft. You can use a counting technique moving from one to ten. Focus on your breath and breathe deeply. As you continue to count higher, move the relaxation down through your body, your shoulders, your chest, down your arms and around your back and buttocks. Feel it as warmth, melting away the stress and tension, and move it down your legs and into your feet. When you reach the number ten, you are totally relaxed and stress-free. You can move the stress and tension down through your heels and into the cushion beneath you, down through the floor and deep, deep down into the foundation of the building and then the center of the earth. Move the stress, tension, anxiety and negativity away from your body. Practice this exercise regularly to obtain a peaceful, serene state. Once the stress, tension and negativity are removed, visualize the healing energy coming into every pore of your body and filling it with a healing peaceful serenity.

Gratitude and appreciation of the small things

The most beneficial emotion we can have is not happiness or joy, which may be short lived; it is gratitude and thankfulness. If you can learn to appreciate the small and wonderful treasures in life, without focusing on the doom and gloom of the world, your information system will be much better served. Some theorists would say that people with a serious or depressive characteristic style are just pragmatic realists; they see the world as it really is. There is some truth to this, but it doesn't work toward any solution. This is like saying "This is who I am; I am incapable of change, take it or leave it." I once spoke with a man who was extremely talented, but had many legal problems and relationship issues. When I asked him what he thought was holding him back, he said: "I have an attitude problem, and I don't want to talk about it."

It really becomes necessary to get outside the box and get a different perspective on a problem if we are going to make a difference. I can commiserate with you and be compassionate to your difficulties, but if you're in the "pity pot," or "under the sewer cover," it doesn't really help you if we all get down in there with you. It is my effort here to demonstrate what you are doing to yourself, to help you to move up and out of the stuck place, but it is necessary for you to reach up to the extended hand, and to realize that you are in need of help. Another individual wanted me to treat all of her family members to "fix" her unhappiness about things in the past. It doesn't work that way. It is only ourselves that we can work on. We cannot make the world smooth and soft; we wear shoes to protect our feet instead. You cannot change others, but you are in control of yourself.

Begin a practice of daily gratitude for small things. Upon awakening, I am immediately thankful for the warm bed I am in. I meditate each morning and then I walk for an extended period while doing the Spring Forest techniques – Small Universe and Self Concentration – which can be found in Appendix 3. These exercises are usually used as sitting meditations but, once you have mastered the concentrated internal movement, the exercises could be applied as a walking meditation movement. Your focus should be on the energy movement through the body; ensure that you walk in a safe environment free from distractions. I walk in a wooded forest preserve where I do not have to worry about traffic. Appreciation for the trees, birds and flowers feeds the soul, grounds me and puts me in the right frame of mind for whatever the day may bring. The practice moves the energy within the body and then utilizes a cleansing action to remove negative energy. If even for a short five-minute period, you can practice a brief meditation to connect with the source of your energy.

Granted, there are days when you cannot bring yourself to see the good in anything. Even in your worst situation, you might be thankful for the benefit of the life lesson you are going through. If you can think of this as a passage, you will remain hopeful about the future.

Diet and nutrition

Your body requires the right chemical balance to survive and function well. Your body mass is composed of approximately 70 percent water, and the electrical processes can be directly affected by a lack of proper hydration. Remember, we are interested in the space between the synapse and the proper chemical environment to have transfer of information.

Drinking soda or coffee is not the best way to hydrate the system. They are not a substitute for water. Water is also a key component in the proper absorption of nutrients in the digestive tract. Make a point to eliminate things from your diet which are not healthy. This includes sugar, white flour products and stimulants such as caffeine. This is especially the case if you are prone to be anxious and nervous. A patient of mine who was depressed was suffering from severe panic attacks occurring at least four times a week. Panic attacks can be very disabling and feeling helpless about them can lead to depression. When we examined the patient's diet, it was dominated by high-caffeinated soft drinks and sugar-filled snacks which were used to provide a quick energy-fix to get through the day. By eliminating these from the diet, and utilizing cognitive behavioral approaches, the panic attacks were eliminated and the depression lifted.

Another patient utilizes the Small Universe breathing and movement to stave off or to recover from a panic attack. When focused on the breathing, after three rounds of the cycle, she has distracted enough from the anxiety to avoid the autonomic nervous system taking over in the flight-or-fight response.

If you have not slept well the night before, it can be very tempting to get a boost from the caffeine coffee drink in the morning. Beware of destructive cycles, like caffeine in the morning and a drink at night to calm down. By practicing qigong, you will not need to rely upon the caffeine for energy. Allow your body to balance itself.

Alcohol is a depressant, and should be avoided, especially if you are taking medication. If you are depressed and using alcohol as a coping mechanism, you are toying with abuse and addiction potential. This is not a road you want to go down; it is only a dangerous side track away from our main goal of health.

Try to eat things that have their own qi still intact. This means it is still fresh and has some life force still in it. Use wholesome foods, locally grown fruits and vegetables and whole grain products as much as you can. Prepare them with the intent of providing a nourishing meal to sustain your body and energy. The Chinese rulers were often careful to have only the highest minded of chefs prepare their meals, transmitting a good qi into the food. Remember to give thanks and offer joy for the food which supports your body functions. Visualize the food nourishing every cell in your body. Even in a busy place, your meal can be a peaceful experience when you enjoy it mindfully.

Relax and be kind to yourself. Get a massage or Reiki treatment to restore your energy field. Sleep can be a form of qigong as well, for when you relax, the body rejuvenates.

Rebounding on the slip ups

If you have a lot of trouble with this process, don't beat yourself up and be self critical. It only adds to the toxic waste, and self loathing takes a lot of energy – energy which you don't have to waste. If you were helping someone to learn to walk again after an accident, or helping a toddler to learn to walk, you wouldn't berate them for making a mistake. They are wiring new neuron connections and it takes time. Be patient with yourself and find the courage to face old patterns, replacing them with more beneficial ones. You need to encourage yourself and simply begin again. Close your eyes and see yourself sweep, sweep, sweeping away the negativity. Don't give up; it is possible to change your mind, your mood and your mental health. You are moving yourself up the ladder of consciousness and breaking the negative automatic patterns of the mind. You are in control, just be persistent. Coach yourself or have someone help you.

The sweeping exercise can be very powerful. One of my daughters is a horse trainer and accomplished rider in hunter-jumper competition. One afternoon, all of her students were having "bad luck" at a horse show. She called and asked me to come immediately to see if I could help. When I got there, everyone was frustrated and really down on themselves for the mistakes they were making. The show was busy and held a great deal of tension and exciting energy. I looked out over the field and spotted a green, grassy hill, away from the tension. We packed up and went over to the hill, about ten of us. I used a relaxation exercise of removing the tension from the body, moving it downward and finally deep into the earth we were sitting on. We used the visualization of the broom, sweep, sweep, sweeping away the negativity and the harsh judgment. Then we went through a visualization of the course, each of them imagining a perfect ride over each jump. Everyone felt relaxed and better afterward. Their performance improved that afternoon, and one of the riders won best in her class, and another took the title of Champion of the Show. So practice sweeping your negativity out of your mind and visualize a "winning" scenario.

· *Chapter 3* ·

Traditional Chinese Medicine and Qigong

Eastern practices of healing through energy manipulation have been growing in acceptance in the West. Much of this has been accomplished through the continued effort of rigorous empirical testing and the medical community's acceptance of acupuncture. The therapeutic intervention of acupuncture is based on the meridian system, as are most energy treatments.

While drinking my tea with breakfast and reading the morning paper, I had the television on. There, to my surprise, was the physician and internationally known author Dr. Christine Northrup on the *Oprah Show* doing a demonstration with the audience about increasing the sensual nature and desire in women. She said, "We need to do some qigong," and everyone stood up, including Oprah Winfrey. Dr. Northrup directed everyone to move qi through the body, by "putting a smile on your face, then move that feeling and smile into your heart, and then moving it down to the lower heart." It was amusing to everyone when Oprah questioned what the "lower heart" was, and Dr. Northrup said, "Well, we can't touch there on television…" Qigong is entering into our mainstream thinking through a variety of venues.

What is qigong?

Qigong is a holistic system of self-healing exercise and meditation, an ancient, evolving practice that includes healing posture, movement, self massage, breathing techniques and meditation (Cohen 1997). Qi is the fundamental "stuff" of the entire manifest universe, the building block of all matter, the basic energy or force that comprises all matter and animates all living things (Reid 1998). It has also been referred to as chi, ki in Japan, or prana in the Hindu tradition, which forms the basis of yoga and Ayurvedic medicine. Qi cannot be detected outside of the form which it takes, but provides the life force or animating force of the matter which it occupies. In our Western sense of reductionism, it may be considered as biomagnetic electrochemical energy. The qigong exercises are similar to tai chi, and they focus on the movement or cultivation of the qi, or life force, through the meridian system.

The word "qigong" was not used in its present specialized sense – "the art of qi cultivation" – until the twentieth century as it related to the martial arts and its application as a force (Cohen 1997). The first book that contained information about qigong was written sometime during early 700 BC. This book was called the *Yellow Emperor's Classic of Internal Medicine* (Carnie 2000). Daoists, who lived austerely in the mountains seeking a deeper truth in nature, practiced and developed many styles of qigong, combining Chinese shamanism and healing with mystical wisdom (Needham 1975). These were spiritual masters who struggled for control of their thoughts and emotions through long meditation to ultimately realize the state of enlightenment or one's "original mind" (Wildish 2000). We can say that the original mind is one without the mistaken beliefs, the mind before socialization. This is the true self, and meditation and qigong can be a useful path to find it.

The state of the original mind was essentially a spiritual condition which allowed an individual to act spontaneously, appropriately and morally in all situations in the everyday world. Psychologically, we may consider this as a change model, much as cognitive therapy creates a greater awareness which allows us to drop our misperceptions of the world. Indeed, meditation is often seen as a complement to psychotherapy, facilitating insight and progress (Epstein 1995). It was Dao (The Way), a social mechanism which allowed one to operate more successfully on a practical basis, long before psychotherapy came to be.

Lengthy meditation practice and concentration required both mental and physical stamina and qigong was developed as a tool to conserve energy or qi and increase longevity. There are different techniques to cultivate the internal qi through sitting meditative practice as well as graceful and slow concentrated movement to keep qi flowing. This reflects the Confucianism philosophy of opposites or yin and yang; in practicing qigong, there is a stillness in the movement, and within the movement, there is a stillness.

Unlike the American expectation that feelings should be voiced, Asians are culturally more apt to keep their thoughts private and there may even be a political danger of speaking one's mind too freely which may result in somaticizing – or holding tension and pain in the body, creating aches and pains. Consequently, each organ function is simultaneously seen as the seat of different emotions (Barnes 1998). In the Western world, a person who is confronted with stress and loss may be likely to become depressed and complain about insomnia, loss of appetite and hopelessness. In China, under similar circumstances, a person is more likely to develop somatic complaints and be diagnosed with neurasthenia (Kleinman 1980, 1986). There are qigong hospitals in China to treat chronic ailments with the qigong techniques.

The meridian system

Qi is believed to flow through tubular systems or channels that radiate beneath the skin (Chan 1987). If you think of your veins carrying blood on a defined roadway, think of these channels like a deer path. They are there, hidden, you only need to look for them. The Chinese acupuncturists have mapped them out after thousands of years of practicing with the different ailments and organs affected. These channels are commonly known as meridians and, when qi is blocked, it will be reflected in the slowing down of the blood flow, which in turn will affect the various organs and the ability of qi to regenerate (Wildish 2000).

Acupuncture is also based upon the flow of qi, with needle placement made along the meridian lines at strategic points as they correspond to the affected area or organ. The curative effects of qigong movements facilitate the flow of qi along the meridian lines, as compared with the concept of meridian points as used in acupuncture practice (Hu 1990). Since a signal grows weaker over the distance of the route, acupuncture points are likened to booster amplifiers (Becker 1990) used to strengthen the signal as it moves along the route. The energy centers, commonly known as the chakras, are very real, and the flow of energy between them has been described, researched and tested at the Menninger Foundation, now in Topeka, Kansas. The clinic was established by Will Menninger to treat mental health patients (Schwarz 1980).

Gap junctions are protein complexes which form channels between adjacent cells which facilitate intercellular communication, increase electrical conductivity and exhibit a high electrical conductance on the body's surface (Bergsman and Wooley-Hart 1973). There is at least one type of differentiated cell called a germ cell which can manifest as tumors and generally concentrate at the seven sites of the chakras (the sites of alchemy energy transfer). This suggests the existence of under-differentiated cells that may be highly interconnected in a normal state as part of the "inner meridian system" and provide important regulatory functions (Nichols et al. 1997). We can't see them, but we know they are there. The meridian and chakra systems not only explain the observations in yoga, acupuncture and qigong, but also successfully predict the research results in conventional biomedical science.

It has been proposed that qi is the result of the resonance of the human body physiological system. Chinese medical literature speaks abut yin qi and yang qi due to molecular transport and electromagnetic wave – the result of electric polarization changes inside the human body as it resonates. The resonance system maintains the coherence of the different physiological functions of the organs inside the body and the efficiency of this system determines the vitality of individual cells as well as the person as a whole (Yeh 1990).

Too much qi or too little qi affects the organs which intersect the meridians (Motoyama 1978). In traditional Chinese medicine, an acupuncturist or qigong practitioner may treat depression along the different meridian lines. A depression related to anger is one that can create a stagnant liver qi, which is different from a depression that comes from grieving over a loss, which manifests in the lungs. If it is a depression due to the absence of qi, the heart becomes the focus, as kidney depression is related to fear (Barnes 1998). This theoretical base of the meridian system is further supported by the finding of more than a dozen-fold, higher-density gap junctions which correspond to the acupuncture points and meridians (Cui 1988; Fan 1990; Mashansky and Markov 1983; Zheng et al. 1996).

Depressed individuals are energetically bankrupt. Their energy has been depleted by closing down the system through blockage. Psychical means for bringing energy to needed sites of the body exist and are intact; however, the energic problems are not of delivery, but of priority (Badalamenti 1985). Stress and high levels of cortisol can tax the system, eventually leading to long-term problems, as we saw earlier with the shrinking of the dopamine receptors. Stress can also lead to problems in the immune function of the body and create illness.

Qi, by its very nature, is related to physical, emotional and spiritual states. Schools of bio-energy practice emphasize the issue of blocked emotions and sometimes spiritual "stuckness" (Barnes 1998). Alternative therapies such as acupuncture and qigong access the mind-body network through the meridian system to release blockage. Qigong breathing exercises aim to increase the capacity of oxygen and qi inhalation and the ability to direct meridian flow and conserve vital energy. There is no distinction between the material and non-material states of qi; qi is as air is and breath is (Wildish 2000) much as we cannot differentiate between the dancer and the dance. The need to identify what the energy or qi is has been less of a priority compared to the need to concentrate on demonstrating to the medical profession that such a power actually exists and that it can indeed exert beneficial healing effects (Wood 1985).

It is important to separate qigong from the traditional Chinese medicine (TCM) diagnosis, which includes questioning of the patient and sophisticated examination for the tongue, eyes and the pulses at the radial artery of the wrist. Qigong may be prescribed by the TCM practitioner. For qigong, diagnosis includes those techniques of TCM together with sensing the body field for blocks of flow of qi; treatments include qigong exercises and, in serious cases, treatment by a qigong therapist or master (Sancier 1999).

A growing body of research indicates that qigong is effective in treating disease, and it is commonly used in both China and Japan as a first choice of treatment for both physical and mental disorders, which they generally view as interconnected. Qigong's techniques and schools also developed in response to influences from Indian yoga and Tibetan Buddhism and are related to tai chi and the martial arts (Reid 1998).

Qigong utilizes conscious breathing and intent, which has been shown to affect the quantity and kind of peptides that are released from the brain stem (Higuchi et al. 1996). With technological advances in our knowledge about how the mind can affect physical and emotional health through neuroendocrine and immunological processes, we may be better able to understand and impact mood disorders and other mental disease, which thus far have been treated on a pharmaceutical and/or cognitive or "consciousness" basis alone. Western science and philosophical discussion have been trying to solve the "mind-body problem" since the time of the philosopher Descartes. Eastern tradition, influenced by Confucianism, has essentially treated the mind and body as unified since it is impossible to have a truly healthy body without a healthy mind and vice versa. This is the basic tenet of the classical Daoist teachings and practical wisdom found in ancient texts (Cleary 1998) and something which Western practitioners are just beginning to learn with integrative medicine.

Qigong, like Western biofeedback therapy, is a systematic training in psycho-physiological self regulation. It is far more pleasant to do than biofeedback, in my opinion. The individual develops skills and intention to regulate the health, balance and movement of the healing energy in the mind and body. These skills have found their way into treatments incorporating mindfulness meditation such as dialectical behavior therapy (DBT) in Western psychology for the borderline personality disorder (Linehan 1993) with superior results over conventional therapy in randomized controlled trials (Linehan *et al.* 1994). DBT was used with severely distressed people and it is done by helping the individual to regulate emotion and the mind, not with medication. I have successfully worked with DBT with numerous patients to help them reach a state of balance without discussion of its basis in the Eastern techniques.

The practice of qigong is meant to activate and balance the various transformations of the physical and spiritual aspects within the various channels and energies of the body. It may serve as a functional link between the energy centers or the chakras. These are described as spinning wheels, which are believed to be located at specific points within the body and which are responsible for the internal alchemy whereby universal essence is transformed into life force energy (Reid 1998). The energy centers and meridians are not perceivable, but more importantly the treatment results correspond to the same patterns or channels between individuals, indicating that they are common to all. Theoretically, qigong is not only a series of manipulations of biological energies, but also a channeling of energies from a universal source (Benor 1997).

Scientists know that each cubic inch of air contains enough energy to power a large city for a very long time. The problem is how to tap that energy source. For our purposes, we need not get hung up on the source of the qi or a scientific breakdown of what it is, but more importantly, we are able to tap it with intent.

There is a spiritual context to the harvesting of qi through your intent to connect with the universal cosmos, but it does not rely upon your belief in any specific religion. It is important that you see yourself as connected with the universe, and a part of it. That is a basic premise of the practice. The initiating affirmation of the Spring Forest exercise is:

I am in the universe. The universe is in my body. The universe and I combine together.

Here we are establishing a connection with all of life force and energy, a basic tenet of the technique. Rather than pulling away from the energy source, and isolating in depression, it is the focus of the intent to connect with the source. This is a powerful spiritual element in the qigong practice.

It is possible to measure the balance of energy at various meridian point junctures by measuring electrical current conductivity at those points. Figure 3.1 shows the contrast between a healthy state and a mentally shocked state of the same person on different days. In this particular example, it is the digestion system (stomach and spleen meridians) which is experiencing an excited condition and the heart and heart constrictor are experiencing a stressed reaction (Figure 3.1).

The symmetry of the energy is disrupted by the stressful experience. As the energy is pulled to one side to accommodate the stress

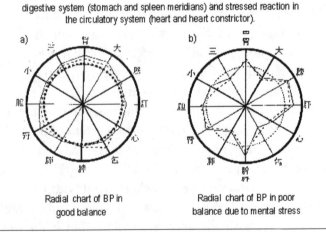

The radial chart of the shocked state indicates excitation of the digestive system (stomach and spleen meridians) and stressed reaction in the circulatory system (heart and heart constrictor).

a)   b)

Radial chart of BP in   Radial chart of BP in poor
good balance   balance due to mental stress

Figure 3.1 Radial charts indicating (a) balance of the system and (b) a stressed state

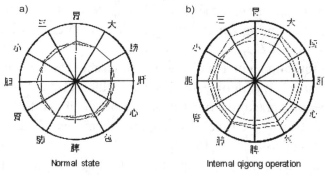

Figure 3.2 Radial charts indicating (a) a normal state and
(b) a greater flow of blood while doing qigong internal exercise

response, it depletes another area and may create a blockage over time with a corresponding illness (Kido 1997).

Figure 3.2 indicates the chart of an individual qigong healer in a state of balance, and the expanded state in the electroconductivity while doing an internal qigong operation. Greater movement was experienced in the energy flow of the meridians, with an increase by 20 percent on average (Kido 1997).

When the energy state in your body is at an optimum level, neither too weak nor too strong, and free flowing, you will experience harmony and good health, even if you encounter stressful situations, as illustrated in my own research presented in Chapter 7. We can encounter countless conflicts and stressors during the day which can manifest a blockage in the meridian system, and a daily practice of qigong is a good tool to maintain a balanced state.

Styles of qigong

There are many different styles and methods of qigong relative to geographic location, sect or family tradition as well as treatment modality, many of which have remained secret (Cohen 1997). In moving or active forms of qigong, the practitioner coordinates breathing and movement in a rhythmic pattern and the mind is focused upon a unified consciousness with the cosmos as well as moving the qi through the body (Huang 1998). This is the basic technique of Spring Forest Qigong Active Exercises, which can be found in Appendix 1.

Identification with the divine and the cosmos can result in grandiosity, and it was during the Boxer Rebellion (1898–1900) that many qigong practitioners died because they believed that qigong and the shamanistic rituals would make them invulnerable to the invaders' bullets (Eserick 1987).

Renee Ryan, one of the qigong practitioners in my study, discussed with our group her experience while studying qigong. During the training in China, while at the back of the room with another Western student, the qi master meant to demonstrate the effects of his qi power. He lifted his hand to transmit the qi or energy into the room. Caught off guard, both she and her fellow student were knocked backwards from their cushions by the force of the energy. The development of the energy was commonly used in the martial arts in China, and so was kept secret, as a weapon might be. Qigong is both an art and a science, and there are a multitude of different techniques for various uses. It is important to understand that the initial roots of qigong come from the martial arts and that the energy of Qi is real and quantifiable. It would be unlikely that anyone would develop the ability to move energy in such forcefulness from doing the health qigong exercises of Spring Forest Qigong.

The complexity of the medical qigong therapy presented a problem for my research study. Master Chunyi Lin developed a simple and convenient method for general health which he called Spring Forest Qigong. The movements combined many of the essential energy-building exercises of more complex styles; it was simple to do and it was available on videotape and audiotape (and is now available on DVD and CD). The Spring Forest Active Practice session takes 40 minutes and could be incorporated into the daily routine of the research subjects without learning a multitude of movements. The CD versions of Small Universe and Self Concentration are about 30 minutes each. Chunyi Lin was also willing to participate in the experiment, transmitting qi to the subjects. The DVDs and CDs are beautifully presented with an easy format to follow. The background music of harp, flute and piano are perfect for visualization of energy moving lightly throughout the body. The different movements and techniques of Spring Forest Qigong which were used in the research study can be found in the Appendices. The exercises found there are the best format to duplicate the treatment application of the research study.

Renee Ryan also uses a technique called Eight Pieces of Silk, which incorporates a qigong movement to dispel grief. While bending at the waist, the person gives the strong sound of "haa" with the tongue extended to expel the stagnant lung qi and the repression of grief. This is a very effective movement when dealing with depression due to loss and grief. For the continuity of the research study, Renee Ryan agreed to the use of the Spring Forest Qigong technique.

There are numerous qigong DVDs available which can be useful to your own practice and specific purpose; some are meant to increase your qi or energy, and some are meant to calm you down. There are specific types of qigong designed for individual treatment. As concluded in the clinical research study, the Spring Forest Qigong exercises for general health are comprehensive and can be very effective in the application to depressive symptoms.

The qigong master and external qi transmission

A qigong master is one who has cultivated and refined the practice and is said to be capable of a transfer of energy by tapping the universal source and acting as a conduit, transmitting healing energy into the systems of their clients through the hands at the point of blockage. This projected form of emitted energy is known as "wai qi" or external qi; it may also refer to the qi that emanates from and surrounds the body which has been called the energetic field of the aura (Cohen 1997). Some masters say they use their own qi, and some say they are tapping a universal qi source.

Emitted qi or qi transference has been documented by Kirlian imaging (Lee 1993; Uchida, Kuramoto and Sugano 1996) and infrared thermovision (Du 1988). The process of electro-photography was researched by Semyon and Valentina Kirlian, who demonstrated the presence of an electrodynamic energy around virtually all forms of matter. The photographs are taken by passing a high-voltage electric current through the object being photographed and the image is captured on film as a glowing corona or aura whose surface sometimes appears to be radiating pencil-like emanations of light. Various advances in the Kirlian method have been extended to include computer imagery and observation of psychological and characterological states which can be detected and measured using the energy field as a resource (Cunningham 1981).

Physiological effects such as respiration, galvanic skin response (GSR), electroencephalogram (EEG) and photoplethysmogram (PPG) have documented the effects of emitted qi (Sakaida et al. 1998). Its effects have been rigorously examined as the literature review indicates. Its mechanisms as a healing agent have been theorized as a form of infrasonic energy corresponding to the formula of nuclear magnetic resonance (Kokubo et al. 1998; Ma 1988). The qi master uses a method of conscious control and intent to direct the healing energy to the recipient (Shen, Tone and Lasayama 1999). Figure 3.3 shows EEG topographies of an individual receiver of wai qi or emitted qi. The changes include an increase in alpha in the frontal area which continued even after the six-minute qi transmission was over. Heart rate and respiration were also measured as slower and stronger.

From this analysis on the brain and autonomic nervous system, it appears that wai qi has effects similar to relaxants, analgesics and even anesthesia and may act to enhance latent healing ability. Since the master is not touching the recipient, it indicates that the energy is transmitted on a transpersonal level through air.

Some qi masters claim to be able to see the energy and blockages as well as feel it with their hands. Master Chunyi Lin reports that he is capable of this skill. My husband, the ultimate cynic, suffers from degenerative disc disease and considerable resulting

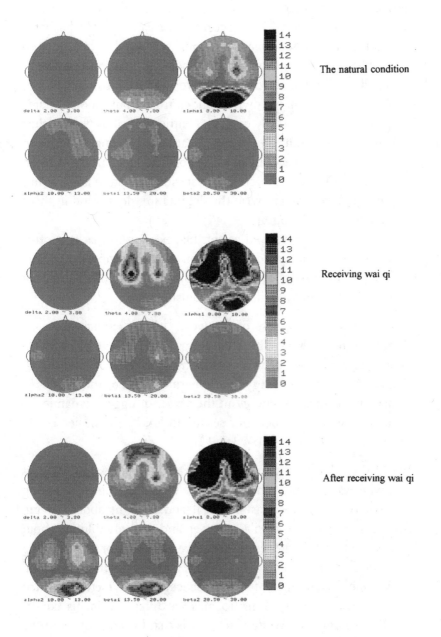

Figure 3.3 EEG topographies of receiver with the eyes closed

back pain. During the three treatment sessions of the study, when the subjects met to record their progress and receive a qi transmission, my husband and I both accepted a treatment. My husband, regretfully, did not continue the qigong practice, but he acknowledges that this was the only time when the pain has ever been alleviated and he remained pain-free for about four months afterward. Arthritis pain in my own shoulder, from an old sports-related injury, was also successfully quelled. Neither one of us was touched by Master Chunyi Lin. This was a remarkable personal experience, and there is much anecdotal evidence of healings, but I was interested to scientifically research the mysterious qi and to apply it in a psychological experiment with the debilitating depression in those who suffer so much from it.

Qigong has been viewed as spiritual healing in that it is often perceived as a mystical and spontaneous recovery, most principally because the mechanism of the mysterious qi is not understood, nor can it be defined in scientific reductionistic terms.

> Problems lie in the use of the word "energy" which has a broader meaning in spiritual healing than it does in physical science, and is likened to organizing principles of vitalism and life force that bring about a harmonizing of the whole person. Healers use energy in the sense to suggest dynamic forces that are channeled or set in motion by the healer, or the patient. (Aldridge 1993, p.13)

One of the subjects in the study came to the first session with his wife, who was a nurse. When we spoke of Chunyi Lin as a qigong master and healer, she was skeptical and thought about leaving with her husband. She didn't, however, and she only told me about her doubt at a later date, expressing her gratitude for what qigong had done for her husband, who was a long-term depressive patient. He was most grateful for the experience and the method, which seemed to be the only thing to make a difference in his condition. Part of our own Western schema is that healing comes in the form of a pill or from an outside intervention. This is our belief system, which is slowly being influenced by our system of scientific proof. Consequently, I ask for you to suspend your cynicism while you give qigong a chance to make a difference in your life. While screening the subjects, another woman said she would not participate in a program that asked her to locate her "third eye," which is an energy center located at the forehead. There was such a strong religious bias that she could not bring herself to get past this minor point.

Measuring qi

Much of the research on qigong has been done in China or Japan. A valuable resource is the Qigong Institute website at www.QigongInstitute.org. The journal articles in most instances have been translated and can be ordered directly from the website. There have been numerous applications of qigong to different medical problems. We don't really know what the mysterious qi is, but there is much evidence of its effect, which can be measured. There has been a significant amount of research directed at EEG measurement of changes relative to qigong treatment and practice in both the subject and the qi master which is of interest.

The synchronization of EEGs between the sender and receiver of wai qi is often found. In a double-blind experiment which excluded the suggestive effects as much as possible, by the master emitting qi from the back of the recipient, synchronizing effects between both EEGs of the master and the subjects indicate the possibility of some information transfer. During hypnosis carried out on the subjects who had already established close rapport with the master, the results were quite different; no synchronized patterns in the topography were evident, indicating something was transmitted transpersonally in the state of wai qi (Kawano 1993, 1998a) (Figure 3.4).

Other studies have been done to show that different states of attention and concentration do not explain this synchronization effect between the qigong sender and receiver (Hearne 1982). Mere visualization differed from that of meditation or qigong practice (Ueda *et al.* 1997). A device for measuring the function of the meridians

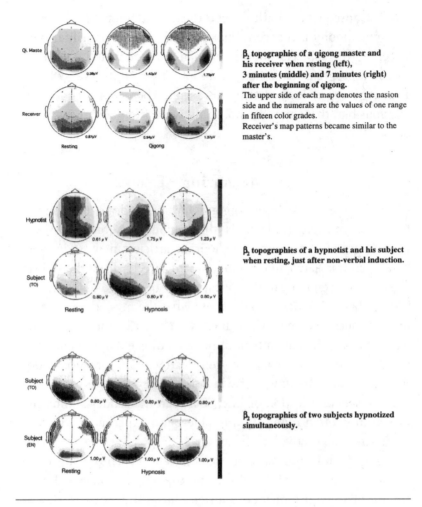

Figure 3.4 The qigong state and hypnosis; during qigong
practice, the topographies of the receiver showed similar
patterns, unlike those of hypnotized subjects

and the corresponding internal organs was developed. The 28 meridian points are monitored to measure skin currents. The apparatus was used to measure remote or distance healing through emitted qi of a master. There were changes reported, and the effects experienced by the receiver of the wai qi differed from those of the placebo effect.

The unknown communication between sender and receiver has been speculated to be merely suggestion. However, a study was undertaken with the sender and receiver separated in two different rooms of a sensory-shielded building, and on different floors, with the qi emission performed at a random time selected by the experimenter. The synchronization phenomena were observed and the right frontal part of the brain exhibited a significant difference between the emitting and non-emitting times in the alpha wave mean amplitudes. The physiological changes strongly suggest the transfer of extrasensory information without suggestion. These studies have been conducted as part of an ongoing study of qigong healing in Japan. The direct effect of conscious intentions on physical systems suggest that mind-consciousness exists and that it has properties and capacities that may not be attributed to the physical and mechanical processes in the brain and nervous system (Rao 1991).

In experiments conducted with qigong masters, skin temperatures of the hands and fingers of both the master and the recipient were monitored by infrared color thermograph. The skin temperature of a trained recipient elevates more readily than that of an untrained recipient, and there is considerable rise in the qigong master after the practice of the dynamic qigong exercise (Ogawa *et al.* 1988).

Thermal imaging of the qi master's palm indicates a change in color and temperature during the state of wai qi or transference of external qi (Huang and Guan 1989) and qi emission can be modulated and self controlled by the consciousness of mind through intent (Du 1988). Emitted qi sent by qigong masters not only includes the energy in the form of infrared ray, static electricity and magnetism, but also is said to affect the molecular structure of matter as well by postulating the maintenance of an "open system" of consciousness with the universe, another open system, and the new theories of quantum physics (Huang 1998).

When a phony qigong master was used, the sham qigong showed no effects on the EEG of alpha bands. So we may conclude that suggestion is not a contributing factor (Tsuda, Sugano and Shirouzu 1999).

The level of practice and expertise is clearly defined by EEG topographic mappings (He, Zhang and Li 1988) and physiological effects may be enhanced by vocalization of certain key words (Machi and Liu 1999). In the Spring Forest Qigong Small Universe technique, the energy is moved while Master Lin's voice indicates a time of movement by certain words – "Ohm" and "Mua." The vagus nerve, which plays a part in the parasympathetic nervous system, can be stimulated by deep breathing exercises and the sound of "Ohm." These, of course, are typical meditative techniques. Activation of the vagus nerve typically leads to a reduction in heart rate, blood pressure or both.

> As sound waves vibrate through the body, crystalline structures within the tissues transform the vibration into pulsed currents. These currents are then conducted to the various corresponding organs and glands, depending on the frequency and amplitude of the incoming wave signal. This tissue transformation (due to wave vibrations) automatically changes the function and flow of energy in the body. Thus, sound vibrations have a profound effect on both human psychology and physiology. Sound or tone resonances have been used for centuries as an effective healing tool and are currently used as an adjunct to modern qigong medicine. (Johnson 2000, p.76)

Externally applied qi immediately decreases beta waves in the brain and simultaneously increases alpha and theta waves. The beta waves (12–30 Hz) are associated with a high level of brain activity as with stress and/or concentration. The theta waves (4–8 Hz) increase with higher-level immune system functioning. Alpha waves have been associated with a healing state of mind (Hole and Estes 1998). The longer the experience of the qigong practitioners, the stronger the alpha waves were, which may indicate the stronger connections of the frontal lobe and the hypothalamo-pituitary, which are making the best of the latent ability of the human brain (Shen et al. 1999).

Group exercise can be especially beneficial, as there is evidence that a qi field is an objective reality which has been detected and measured (Lu, Wang and Yan 1988). A group of qigong amateurs were exercising in a room which was measured with an instrument sensitive to gamma-rays and thermal neutrons over a three-and-a-half-hour period of time on four different occasions. The measurements were compared to the measurements of the empty room. The electromagnetic field was not an influence on the measurement. The measurements were significant to indicate the evidence of a qi field which was existent at the time of the exercise and after the students left the room.

In measuring changes in EEG with progression of qigong training over a 12-month period, the ratio of the frontal to the occipital alpha waves tended to increase with practice (i.e. the ability to maintain a deeper state of relaxation occured over time), and at the twelfth month, it became larger during qigong than in resting (Kawano 1998a). *This would indicate that the benefits increase with time and consistency of practice.* The EEG alpha frequency increases during qigong practice and, even in the resting state, alpha for qigong practitioners is greater than the average person, corresponding to that of Buddhist meditators, such as Transcendental Meditation (TM); however, the theta-type waves are different (Kawano, Shi and Duan 1996). With longer training periods, the ratio of the alpha waves on the frontal to the occipital regions becomes larger (Kawano *et al.* 1997). Length of practice indicates that greater change can occur over time, so you can expect to see more benefits the longer you practice. I would suggest that you do at least a 40-minute practice on a daily basis, if possible.

Therapeutic Touch (TT) is a technique that is actively taught to nurses and medical professionals in the West, which may be compared to qigong in some aspects. TT is a non-invasive healing modality which was originally derived from the ancient healing practice of the "laying on of hands" and is normally performed with the hands held at a distance of 2–6 inches from the patient's body (Kreiger 1990; Lionberger 1985). TT can significantly alter the physiology of the individual treated when measured with electromyographic analysis (EMG) in consideration of the Eastern concept of "nadis" or chakras. It was also reported that a compassionate desire to heal resulted in a physiological change which is particularly evident in the heart chakra region (Wirth and Cram 1993). When an analysis of EEG function was done between meditation and TT healing mental states, they were found to be differentiated (Brown et al. 1977).

The blood

Qigong has been shown to affect the brain blood supply by increasing the blood flow of the brain vessels (Dou and Zhang 1989) and could therefore enhance the therapeutic benefits of drugs allowing for reduced sick leave, dosage, duration of hospitalization and costs of therapy (Sancier 1999). Given an increase in brain blood supply and an enhanced ability to concentrate through the continued use of qigong, health and intelligence are said to have been affected by showing an increase in the mathematic ability of students (Guan 1989) and qigong has been proposed as a method of reform in schools (Huang and Huang 1989). Blood flow in the meridians and the vascular system of a qigong master is higher than other persons without qigong practice (Guo 1993), as is the white blood cell count (Shibata and Furiya 1993).

We have already discussed the relationship between qigong and energy metabolism, especially as it relates to ATP, the energy currency of the mitochondria. Endocrine and immune response during qigong meditation have also been evaluated. Sympathetic nerve activity decreases, the stressors are reduced, and the level of brain activity decreases in qigong meditation (Higuchi et al. 1996). You are in the relaxation response mode in the qigong state.

Positive emission tomography (PET) and regional cerebral blood flow (rCBF) images indicate that there is a general reduction of blood flow in the right amygdala which is correlated with both EEG theta and alpha, and the left hippocampus with delta, which supports the idea that qigong practice produces a unique state of mind and documents the effects of psychological relaxation (Itoh,

Miyazaki and Takahashi 1996). The amygdala is a strong response center of anger and emotion in the brain, part of the limbic system, which is a part of our early evolutionary development. Hence, qigong may be considered as a treatment for anger management. The stress-related hormones of glucocorticoid and cortisol are positively affected by qigong exercise (Jiang and Tao 1989).

Structure changes of distilled and mineral water before and after qi irradiation were investigated and it was found that the irradiated water became a so-called "healthy water" (Adachi *et al.* 1998). In an effort to determine the ability of matter to store the energy, the electric conductivity of water was measured before and after qi transmission. A certain qi "respiration" phenomena occurred over time (Shigemi 1994). As the body is mostly made up of water, qi may affect not only the energy system, but also the basis of the body's structure.

Increases in qi flow and blood circulation help nourish diseased or stressed tissue, providing a means for the body to heal itself. When clinical studies were reviewed to illustrate the improvement of health and the benefit of qigong, it was found that there was a positive effect on mortality, stroke and hypertensive patients and blood pressure, improvement in sex hormone levels and an enhanced activity of an anti-aging enzyme which destroys free radicals that may cause aging (Sancier 1996). Since blood pressure is noted to drop in the receiver of wai qi, it was used as a measure in my research study to indicate if, indeed, there was evidence of a transfer of energy from the qigong master to the subject. Registered nurses were present to take the blood pressure of each subject before and after the energy transmission. There were general indications of a drop in blood pressure after the individual 10-minute treatment session, with some as many as 20 points.

The nervous system and neuro-endocrine system

Relaxation and tranquility are a main foundation of the qigong practice. When you relax your body, you enter a healing and restorative state. Your immune system is the direct beneficiary of the qigong practice. When you experience the relaxation response, you are better able to maintain a more balanced state of mind, and deal with problems in a more responsive way rather than impulsively.

We have already covered the effects on serotonin and dopamine in the material in Chapter 2 on the information system. Qigong has been successfully integrated with psychotherapy in the treatment of anxiety and hypertension (Mayer 1998). In a preliminary evaluation of qigong treatment of eight patients who met the *Diagnostic and Statistical Manual–III* (DSM-III: American Psychiatric Association 1980) criteria for anxiety, the Hamilton Rating Scale was also used to evaluate the mental state of the patients. The therapeutic effect was found to be 87.5 percent with this small sample. Five patients were cured and two improved; one patient failed to respond to the qigong exercise. The findings in this case were that qigong is similar to Jacobson's relaxation exercise and progressive relaxation or systematic desensitization exercises (Shan *et al.* 1989). These are all commonly used interventions for anxiety.

Beneficial effects of qigong have been reported on such psychosomatic and emotionally rooted disorders such as irritable bowel syndrome (IBS), premenstrual distress, chronic non-biologic psychogenic pain, migraine, eating disorders and chronic low-back syndrome. It has also been used to access and release suppressed and repressed emotion, and sometimes memory of debilitating early life events, which have led to positive behavioral changes (Pavek 1988).

It has even been reported that qi properties can readily enter the tape of a music cassette which is coated with zinc and iron oxide, creating physiological responses and pain reduction in those who are exposed to the healing music (Nishimoto 1996). Pain was said to have been reduced by 73.6 percent when compared to a control group. Omura (1990) also claimed that drug uptake was increased by using "qigongized paper," which was applied to an afflicted area such as a spastic muscle, reducing or eliminating the pain.

When individuals enter the qigong state, activities of their visual cortex and pathways are decreased. As the sense organs are the main gatekeepers of mind and body, inhibition of distraction promotes a deeper state of meditation and focused concentration which results in improving a person's resistance and ability to endure stressful situations more effectively. Qigong has been shown to functionally affect the sympathetic excitability of electric potentials (Cao, Zhao and Zhang 1989) – the basic mechanism of the information highway.

The inhibition occurring during the qigong state is different from that in sleep. The potential for the physiological mechanism of muscle relaxation and strengthened muscle force were positively affected in the qigong state (Liu et al. 1988). The cortical inhibition has obvious effects on the nervous system and the results share similar features of sleep and meditation, but are also different (Peng and Liu 1988). The brain stem which controls many of these functions is directly affected.

It is believed that qigong is effective in eliminating stress and improving the immune responses. When endocrine and immune responses were measured in cancer patients before and after a 40-minute qigong exercise, the level of plasma cortisol and adrenaline decreased, but B-endorphin, dopamine, noradrenaline, CD4/CDS and Natural Killer (NK) cell activity had a tendency to increase (Higuchi et al. 1997). What this means is that the bad information decreased, and the good information increased. Based on the fact that plasma cortisol and adrenaline decreased, it is presumed that qigong alleviates stress and decreases the sympathetic nerve activity. Also, based on the fact that the NK cell activity improved, it is presumed that qigong elevates immune responses.

Qigong can induce a slow reversible depolarization of sodium channels and could increase the peak current by more than 39.7 percent (Liu et al. 1989; Liu, Zhao and Du 1993). The sodium channels are part of the information system mechanism, so the potential for greater transmission is occurring. With qigong, you are essentially "pumping up" the mechanism.

The information system is directly and positively affected by the qigong state. Through the use of intent, focused attention and cognitive awareness of your negative thoughts, you can change your thinking and your mental health. This is a basic part of the psychotherapy process. You can enhance and speed your recovery from depression by doing a consistent qigong practice.

Qigong deviation syndrome/qigong psychotic reaction

The DSM-IV (American Psychiatric Association 1994, p.847) recognizes a culture-bound syndrome of qigong psychotic reaction when individuals become overly involved in practice. It is described as an "acute, time-limited episode characterized by dissociative, paranoid, or other psychotic or non-psychotic symptoms." The diagnosis is also included in the *Chinese Classification of Mental Disorders*, second edition (CCMD-2), and is known as qigong deviation syndrome. None of the patients in my research study experienced any ill effects from doing the Spring Forest Qigong exercise, and the bipolar patients were evaluated and monitored by me between the regular monthly meeting sessions. When done properly, I consider qigong to be a low-risk method to treat depressive symptoms.

Simple precautions should be taken when using qigong, as it affects the neurochemistry of the body. You need to make your practice practical and sensible. It is best to use a prescribed protocol, and to do the exercise for a limited period each day. Don't go overboard, thinking that more will be better. A daily practice of qigong is meant to bring balance to your system, not to overwhelm it. Follow the directed practice protocol and be sure to "harvest the qi" at the end of the session back to the lower dantian, which is located behind your navel. You do this by moving your hands in a clockwise manner over the navel and visualizing the energy there.

In a study of 109 patients with mental disorders caused by qigong psychophysical exercise (Shan *et al.* 1989), the patients were divided into schizophrenic type (47) and neurotic type (62) and they were analyzed by standard psychiatric rating scales and the Minnesota Multiphasic Personality Inventory (MMPI), a standard personality test. The results showed that patients with qigong deviation presented abnormalities in perception, thinking, emotions and behavior of varying degree which could not be diagnosed as another functional mental disease and was felt to be related to the adverse flow of qi or vital energy. The mean scores of these patients were not correlated to clinical diagnosis. Most of the patients manifested specific physical symptoms, and it was felt that qigong could trigger certain latent tendencies (Shan *et al.* 1989) which existed before doing the exercise.

The qigong deviants were more suggestible, dependent, hypochondriac and easily distracted, showing much more concern about their physical functions and may have manifested hallucinations. Delusions were limited to qigong topics (Shan *et al.* 1989). Any so-called qigong-induced psychoses may be more appropriately labeled qigong-precipitated psychoses, where the practice of qigong acts as a stressor in vulnerable individuals (Ng 1999). Qigong-induced health disturbances are believed to arise from the inappropriate application of qigong, incorrect regulation of the mind to reach the tranquil state or to control respiration and/or the inability to terminate qigong (Ng 1999).

It is recommended that at the end of every practice one should finish with "shou gong," a moment designed to bring all the qi back to the elixir field and store it there; this procedure will also make the practitioner calm and relaxed (Tse 1995). In the Spring Forest Qigong, this is done by focusing on the lower dantian, behind the navel, and moving the hands over it in a clockwise direction as indicated.

Different techniques and training methods may not be compatible with the individual's constitution and physique and qigong deviations may ensue (Zhang and Xu 1997). The number of qigong-induced mental disorders has been rising in China and there are now special clinics to treat such cases (Ng 1999).

A study of 28 cases of qigong deviation was assessed with the Minnesota Multiphasic Personality Inventory-2 (MMPI-2). Compared with a group of 27 normal persons, and another group of 29 qigong practitioners who had not experienced deviations, the group with qigong deviations scored high on the following subscales: hypochondriasis, depression, hysteria and psychopathic deviate (Xia and Lin 1996).

Psychological effects of motor phenomena and perceptual changes such as experience of warmness, chilliness, itching sensation in the skin, numbness, soreness, bloatedness, floating, dropping, enlargement or constriction of the body image, and formication were experienced, but deemed as transient and vanished as the exercise terminated (Xu 1994). Inappropriate training is also a factor, and a blind self-taught exercise is accountable for 67.8 percent of qigong deviation (Shan et al. 1989). Physiological effects include changes in the EEG, EMG, respiratory movement, heart rate, skin potential, skin temperature and finger tip volume, sympathetic nerve function, function in the stomach and intestine, metabolism and endocrine and immunity systems (Xu 1994).

Emotional changes such as crying, laughing, shouting or dancing have been experienced as "spontaneous dynamic qigong" (SDQ) and is more common in females. In a study utilizing the MMPI, it was determined that neither the qigong trainees nor the instructors represented a special group of the population prone to hysteria (Wu and Xu 1988). It was hypothesized that the SDQ may be a result of the release of the body's symbolic manifestation of unconscious repressed material. The clinical phenomena are very similar to anxiety disorder, conversion disorder, dissociative disorder, obsession disorder, schizophrenia and other psychotic conditions (Ng 1999).

Those with qigong-induced mental disorders were different from schizophrenia sufferers by their age of onset, etiology, symptomology and treatment response as well as prognosis (Wu 1992). Most cases recovered after one or two months, while a few had a protracted course and recovered after one to two years (He 1996). Reactions are also treated by psychiatrists using a combination of medications and psychological interventions. Especially vulnerable are individuals who become overly involved in the practice or who practice intensively. As with any medication, too much of a good thing can create problems, and more is not necessarily better.

Qigong practice should not exceed three hours (Zhang and Xu 1997); much as the finding that over-meditation can cause serious emotional disturbance and hallucinations (West 1979). As an altered state of consciousness, qigong may encourage the initial use of dissociation as a defense and pave the way for dissociative behaviors (Ng 1999).

Kundalini is essentially the energy consciousness which is said to flow through the chakras and remains "coiled like a serpent" in its unawakened state (Hills 1990; Wilber 1990). Meditation and energy manipulation have been associated with Kundalini-rising experiences, which may lead to ego inflation or a premature transcendence creating physical and emotional symptoms (Bailey 1990; Harris 1994). I have successfully treated such cases.

To avoid any anxiety about your qigong regimen, I recommend that you begin with the Spring Forest Small Universe exercise, and the Active Exercises. You want to first begin by moving the energy in the torso with the Small Universe technique, and then use the Active Exercises to move the energy through the meridians down the limbs to open all the channels. The technique, when used as directed, is safe and has been tested in the research study with the participants suffering from depression.

Other treatment applications

Qigong has been evaluated as an effective treatment for stress management (Dockstader and Barrett 1998; Lim 1988) and post-traumatic stress disorder (Hutton, Liebling and Leire 1996).

The release of catecholamines (Cas) has been associated widely with stress, and the excretion of urinary Cas is a useful index of the activity of the sympathetic-adrenal medulla system. In a study of 111 subjects, urinary adrenaline (A) and noradrenaline (NA) were measured during qigong and a controlled rest. Excretion of both urinary A and NA increased, and amounts were directly correlated to the length of experience (Tang and Sun 1989). As a stress coping method, qigong affects and plays a role in hormonal regulation related to the maintenance of homeostasis.

Qigong is less strenuous and methodical than yoga or qigong's martial arts cousin, tai chi, and it may be more accessible to sick and elderly people. Its physiological effects of deep breathing and relaxation are similar to the "relaxation response" of Harvard's Dr. Herbert Benson (Stone 1997). Qigong has been shown to reduce the number and need of different medications as therapeutic remedies (Reuther and Aldridge 1998; Sancier 1999). Qigong emphasizes preventative medicine and patients may be encouraged to take responsibility for their own health.

In treatment for heroin drug addiction, it was shown to significantly reduce withdrawal symptoms and measurement of anxiety scores, as well as reduce the period of time of positive readings from the urine as compared with a control group (Li, Chen and Mo 1999). Qigong has also been an effective agent in anesthesia (Machi and Zhong 1996), although it is not completely understood. The dependence of the outcome on the intent of the qigong master has profound implications for medical qigong in clinical applications as reported with cell growth factors on sperm cells, DNA and protein synthesis (Sancier 1990).

Electroacupuncture has been used for the treatment of depression, accelerating the synthesis and release of serotonin and norepinephrine with clinical findings at least as effective as treatment with amitriptyline (Han 1986; Yang, Liu and Jia 1994), and qigong may prove to be an effective agent as well. A case study of bipolar disorder and the therapeutic use of qigong and traditional Chinese medicine, including acupuncture, is reported to have reduced the daily dose of lithium in half and the more balanced feeling had remained stable for five years (Bassman 1997).

When qigong therapy was applied in patients with arteriosclerotic obstruction, a therapeutic effectiveness rate of 83.3 percent was reported for subjective symptoms such as cold leg or leg pain; 90 percent for a rise in the leg temperature measured by thermography; 72.4 percent for improvement in a plethysmograph; and 64.7 percent for improvement in the peripheral blood flow by an ultrasonic Doppler flow measure (Agishi 1996).

When combined with a biofeedback apparatus, qigong uses the advantages of both Western and Eastern techniques in regulating the autonomic nervous system. It has been used for psychological training before athletics, relaxation training of exam anxiety, enhancing concentration and learning potential, as well as improving qigong skills (Qin et al. 1989). When qigong therapy was used with university students diagnosed with neurasthenia, improvement was seen in sleep and mental and emotional functions (Qin et al. 1989). In a study of healing qigong maneuvers which measured the strength of muscles through resistance over time, it was found that the qigong master could both weaken and strengthen the muscle through intent, even when flashcards were shown to the subjects with the opposite command of "weak" or "strong" (Sancier 1990).

Analysis of the DNA mass of tumor treated by qigong indicates that mass was lower than that in a control group, directly proportional to the frequency of treatment (Feng, Qian and Peng 1998). Qi may act as a scavenger of hydroxy radicals and protect nerve cell membranes (Tang et al. 1993). In a study which applied qigong techniques as an auxiliary therapy for Parkinson's disease (PD), after one year of practicing, the Webster's marks of 52 PD patients decreased remarkably; the mean decrease was 18.4 percent. For the control group, the Webster's marks of 31 PD patients who took only medicine increased slightly without significance. The difference of the change between the qigong and the control groups was significant and indicated that combining qigong therapy further improved the clinical conditions more than simple pharmacotherapy did (Yu et al. 1998).

When time experiments were conducted to clarify what actions qi energy has on the capacity for cancer cells of lymph corpuscles in human blood, it was found that it increased the capacity for monocytes containing natural killer cells. It raised the concentration of intracellular calcium ions in human neutrophiles and it heightened phagocytosis (Kataoka, Sugiyama and Matsumoto 1997). This means the energy has an effect for improving the function of human cell immunity activity and suggests it may provide a natural and complementary therapy for cancer.

Qigong may have an effect on personality. In measurements with the Eysenck Personality Questionnaire (EPQ) and a Type A Behavior Pattern Questionnaire (TABP) over a two-year period, it was shown that neuroticism scales and TABP scores were lowered in the persistent practitioners (Tang and Wei 1993). The lower scores on the TABP were also seen in another two-year study which utilized the Symptom Checklist-90 (SCL-90). Significant improvement in mental health functioning measured by psychosomatic symptoms was displayed in the qigong group over a control group (Wang 1993). Mentally, the patients practicing qigong became healthier and more balanced.

Qigong has also been used to enhance learning ability and improve concentration. In a one-year study with 170 fourth-grade students (nine and ten year olds), qigong exercises were utilized during class periods. For comparison purposes, a control group was established. The average test scores of members of the qigong groups showed an increase of 11.9 percent, and the scores of the control group did not change. Several disruptive students were reported to show dramatic increases as their memory and behavior improved (Tong and Xe 1990). This may have implications for treatment of attention deficit hyperactivity disorder (ADHD). In qigong practitioners, the speed and accuracy of memory was significantly improved in digit span performance and reading colors with interference of words, such as black-red number (Wang 1988).

As external qigong is used as a method of medical care, physiological measurements of qigong anesthesia have been made in surgical operations and in stopping pain. EEG, electrocardiogram (ECG) and galvanic skin responses (GSR) were measured for both the qigong master and the patients. The master applied the external qigong to the "yin tang," an area which is located between the eyebrows. The "synchronization phenomenon" was observed and was seen in the alpha wave region of EEG topographs. Heart rate changes for both persons were also experienced (Machi and Chu 1996).

The studies show that the qigong exercise may be superior to physical exercise such as calisthenics. When qigong was compared with cycling for respiratory patterns and EEG, similar physiological effects were observed. The qigong respiration rate was suggestive of hyperventilation; however, it was felt that the EEG changes were unlikely to be the result of hyperventilation since they were not characteristic of hyperventilation's fluctuating increase of bilaterally synchronous slow activity and slowing of alpha and beta rhythm (Sim and Grewal 1989).

Exercise has long been a staple prescription for those who suffer from depression, and studies have suggested that it is almost as effective as antidepressants in relieving depression. A new study has found that, even though people who exercise are less likely to be depressed or anxious, it is probably not because they exercise (De Moor *et al.* 2008). This twin study found that the reduction in depressive symptoms could be explained genetically. People disinclined to exercise also tend to be depressed. One does not cause the other. Exercise may still be beneficial, but there was no causal effect. As qigong is a less rigorous routine, it is likely to be more consistently practiced.

· Chapter 4 ·

Identifying
Your Problem

Everyone feels sad at times and most people can shake it off after a few days. Clinical depression, or unipolar depression, affects approximately 15 million American adults. It is a serious condition, and should not be taken lightly. If you or a family member suffers from depression, it needs to be addressed as soon as it manifests. Earlier, in Chapter 2, we discussed the information system and how your thoughts can affect the neurochemistry of your brain. Thoughts can have an impact, but depression can occur from a combination of factors. Let's look at some of them.

Causes of depression

Genetics

Certainly, genetics is a key factor in the risk for depression. When someone comes in with symptoms of depression, one of the first questions I might ask will be concerning a family history of depression. Sometimes it is not always evident because the ancestor may not have been diagnosed or treated for the illness. Perhaps they used a substance such as alcohol instead, or they were always irritable and angry. Earlier research has indicated a genetic link for depression, and now that molecular genetic techniques are available, there is even greater interest to identify which chromosomes are affected. In the future, it is foreseeable that many mental disorders might be treated by adjustment to the genetic mechanisms of the individual. This is a leap of progress in removing the stigmatism of having a mental illness, and a long way from how people with emotional disorders were treated in the past.

When considering your family pedigree, it is important to remember that, just because you have a close family member that was diagnosed with depression, it does not necessarily mean that *you* have the genetic markers. I would also advise you to recall the study by the Benson team, discussed earlier, which showed that qigong, through the relaxation response, could "switch off" certain genes which were responsible for emotional dysfunction (Dusek *et al.* 2008). Your genetic history is not a lifetime sentence.

Biochemistry

A deficiency or surplus of the two neurotransmitters, serotonin and norepinephrine, can result in depressive symptoms. This can occur because your body simply isn't making enough – through a genetic deficiency – or because of some other reason. It could be your thought patterns, but it could also be due to substance. This is especially true in the world of recreational drugs. If you have tampered with the delicate balance of your brain chemistry by taking recreational drugs, tragic consequences can result.

The popular Rave drug Ecstasy, known as the "hug-drug," floods the system with serotonin and the individual experiences a feeling of euphoria. Ecstasy will deplete the body of the available serotonin, body temperature rises, and, in some instances, death can occur. But a further problem comes a few days later when the mood plummets and depression sets in. Typically, this has been identified as "suicide Tuesdays," a disastrous fallout of the party weekend scene. If you continue this yo-yo mood manipulation, you could be heading for a lifelong problem with bipolar depression. Feel-good drugs have long-term consequences and are best left alone. If you have used drugs, qigong can assist your program of ongoing recovery if coupled with diet, detoxification and therapy. Qigong can help to rebalance your body's natural energy resources.

Some prescribed medications for illness such as heart disease or cancer can trigger depression. Hypothyroidism – a condition of an underactive thyroid – could also be responsible for depressive symptoms. A physical examination by your doctor to rule out such medical problems is always advised.

You may experience depression as a result of a medical condition or illness, as well as a compounded or secondary depression which is substance induced by taking a prescribed medication.

Environmental elements

Trauma is a well-known cause of depression. This can be something which is emotional or physical. Medical illness, financial problems, loss of employment or a loved one and abuse – sexual, emotional or physical – can all be related to a feeling of helplessness and hopelessness which catapults the individual into depression. If you are in a difficult relationship with someone, you may want to seek couples therapy or seriously rethink the commitment as it relates to your well-being. Co-dependency can be a precipitator to depression, often seen in the form of dysthymia. The co-dependency term comes initially from the alcoholism treatment model. This is where the whole family is "co-dependent" and move around the elephant in the room, the alcoholic. No one wants to deal with the problem directly, so they adjust their own lives to keep the family secret. As a result, the family dynamics are dysfunctional and communication is "closed." This model can be applied to a number of different scenarios such as abuse, promiscuity or workaholism. The co-dependent serves to enable the dysfunctional system and the dependent behavior by not asserting themselves. This avoidance results in a mild depression which comes and goes, known as dysthymia. It can manifest into a full-blown clinical depression, depending upon circumstances and genetics.

Economic and environmental factors of the world situation have a strong effect on many individuals who are sensitive and susceptible to negative events. If you are one of these people, I would advise you to refrain from becoming a news junkie and retreat from the late evening news. Images of floods, disasters and plummeting stock prices are not the type of visualizations you want playing center stage in your brain before sleep. After the 9/11 disaster in New York, millions of people were traumatized by the continuous replaying of the scene of airplanes crashing into the World Trade Center. I am not suggesting that you ignore such world events, but that you put a space or distance between you and the scene.

Occupational issues can be especially problematic because you need your job to maintain your livelihood. If you have a work overload, a lack of control over your job function, or you have a conflict between your personal life and your duties, stress and frustration can easily lead to depression. Once again, it is the feeling of hopelessness that becomes the pivotal point. Corporate reorganization and technological change in the workplace that are seen as outside the control of the individual are major components in causes of depression.

There is a strong cyclical connection between anxiety and depression. Anxiety is a fear-based emotion, as is anger. An anxious-reactive person may experience the fear after the stressor has been removed. For instance, if you left your job because your boss was a tyrant, or perhaps you were downsized, you might fear having another bad employer or losing your job at the hands of yet another restructure. The stressor is viewed as challenging or threatening, and the individual responds with apprehension and insecurity. This is the commonly known flight-or-fight response of the body. Worry and rumination create an increase in the level of stress-related neurotransmitters. The thought processes and the body become so connected as to be automatic, responding to any cue in the environment which is similar, and this can lead to anxiety disorders such as generalized anxiety disorder (GAD) or panic attacks. It can then become a self-perpetuating anxiety reaction. An aversive attitude to change sets in; the individual begins to limit the challenges and experiences depression because it appears hopeless. The body and the adrenals are running the program on autopilot. The cure is to exercise courage and do exactly the opposite of what your fear is telling you. This, of course, is if the fear is unreasonable. If there is a real threat from someone at your workplace, that is a different scenario. Change is the only constant in our world, and the more comfortable you become with it, the better you will navigate the inevitable transitions which life presents. Qigong can help to assist you in maintaining the proper balance of the body through the change.

Gender and age

Women will experience depression twice as often as men. This may not be because they are more susceptible to depression, but that they report it more often, or present for help in the treatment setting. Men will tend to tough it out and not seek treatment because the cultural demands of Western society mistakenly identify this as a weakness. Men will more often distract themselves with physical activity or watching television or perhaps by drinking alcohol.

In women, hormonal changes, pregnancy, childbirth and menopause are all considered in the proper diagnostics of depression. Some women may devote too much of themselves to family and others, negating their own desires and sense of self. If you are a caretaker and neglect your own ability to support yourself, it can be particularly devastating to be left to fend for yourself after divorce or bereavement. This is more common than we would like to see. It is a problem of learned helplessness. Gender models for partners (their mothers and fathers) have historically been the full-time homemaker, housewife or stay-at-home mom, and the man as sole breadwinner. In today's economic times, women usually work and take care of the home. More pressure is put on the marital relationship which does not meet the model of our parents and, many times, we don't understand why until it is examined in therapy. Unrealistic expectations in marriage are the number one cause of marital discord.

Women tend to dwell on things, ruminating more, and over-thinking issues. There is an evolutionary structural reason for this.

The corpus callosum of women is 50 percent larger than that of men. This is the part of the brain which connects the cortex of the two cerebral hemispheres. Because historically women were the gatherers, searching the ground for edibles, they developed this part of the brain to scan better. Men were the hunters and had to travel long distances from home. They were focused on getting the meat and bringing it home. If you think about this in modern terms, this is why women go into the store and shop, scanning the racks and spotting what matches items in their closet. Men will go in, get what they need and get out. A larger corpus callosum works for women in terms of multiple tasking activities and against women in that they will continually rehash the scenario from left to right sides of the brain. Anxiety mounts and depression can follow.

An example of this was when my husband and his crew of men lost a set of keys to a truck on the way to a new location. The keys were left on the hood of the car and, when the car was driven away, they slid off. It was only a matter of blocks, but the men looked for hours up and down the street. At the end of the day, feeling frustrated, my husband came home and told me the story of their efforts. We ate dinner and then I said, "Well, let's take another ride and see if I can spot them." He laughed and said, "We have been looking the *whole* day, Fran." Being persistent, I cajoled him into trying again. Within 200 yards of the trip, I spotted them lying on the ground near the sidewalk. On the other hand, I can toss and turn worrying about something at night, while he sleeps peacefully.

As we get older, our beauty fades and perhaps our health. If your identity is tied up in remaining youthful, perfectionism can be a cruel task master and you are bound for disappointment with yourself. You need to learn to love and accept yourself as worthy. People who place their value on what they do and how they look have set themselves on a never-ending treadmill of dissatisfaction. To be at peace with your age is a worthy goal, and remember that each age has its own benefits.

Post-partum depression is also becoming something which we have become more aware of, and which is often misunderstood. In post-partum depression, there is a fluctuation of hormones, and this illness tends to have genetic components. It is distinguished from a normal baby blues reaction by the duration as well as some of the more debilitating symptoms. Having a child should be a joyful event, but when depression sets in, a cycle of guilt and negativity create a detachment from the child. Don't ignore the symptoms because of guilt; talk with your spouse and doctor about what you are experiencing.

Depression in older people is closely associated with the loss of independence, a life partner as well as disability. Seniors are also the least likely to seek treatment, often feeling ashamed of their loneliness and isolation and fearing transitions to assisted living arrangements. A strong support structure is important for elders and can enhance family connection.

Men and women react differently to depression. As indicated previously, women are more likely to seek treatment and to internalize the problems. They feel bad about themselves, taking the blame for their situation and withdraw. They might talk with a friend or therapist. Men do not wish to be seen as weak; our culture does not allow it, and men are prone to take action. Men will more often than not act out or abuse alcohol. They may be irritable, argumentative or tend to work more and disengage. Withdrawal and isolation are common denominators to both men and women.

Cognitive

Someone who has a pessimistic personality style may be considered as a pragmatic realist. But there are extremes. Much as we would not want a superficial "Pollyanna" style, we don't want to be a doom-and-gloom naysayer. A personality style is different than a disorder. A personality disorder exists when the characteristic style is affecting three areas of your life in a negative manner.

The three areas we look at when diagnosing a personality disorder are how the style affects the social, work and intimacy components of life. Intimacy is the most difficult, and does not necessarily mean sexual intimacy. This is the ability to be close and open with others. It requires a certain comfort with vulnerability. Work is the easiest task to master. If you lost your job, which is where most of your social connection exists, and then you had difficulty relating to your spouse, you are experiencing a composite deficit in all three areas. Depression could set in, depending upon your ego strength, support structure and flexibility to deal with the situation.

If you have low self esteem, are avoidant, critical, brooding and given to worry as a pervasive characteristic pattern or style, you may have what is known as depressive personality disorder. This pattern will usually develop into dysfunctional relating, and depressive symptoms. When I ask this type of person what they want in life, they will usually respond in the negative – such as "I don't want to lose my job again," or "I don't want a cheating husband." This is a fear-based response. The challenge here is to create a new way to relate to events on a cognitive basis. We need to look at the schema, or how data are filtered, and reframe or rewire the information system with a more open and positive outlook. This may be a long process, because the style is more pervasive and of long duration, but it is possible. It is more easily done with doing the qigong practice.

Symptoms of depression

There are several symptoms of depression, including the following:

- lack of interest or pleasure in activities you once enjoyed, including sex

- persistent sadness, restlessness, anxiousness, irritability and/ or tension

- changes in appetite with significant weight loss or gain, not due to dieting

- sleeping too much or too little, insomnia and waking in the middle of the night or early morning hours, unable to fall asleep again

- loss of energy or increased fatigue

- feelings of worthlessness, hopelessness or inappropriate guilt

- difficulty thinking, concentrating, remembering or making decisions

- thoughts of self harm or preoccupation with death; suicidal ideation

- persistent physical symptoms such as chronic pain or digestive disorders that do not respond to treatment.

If you are experiencing several of these depressive symptoms and they last longer than a few weeks, and interfere with your normal functioning, you are likely suffering from some form of depression and should seek professional treatment. You could also take up a daily program of the qigong exercises presented in this book.

I would like to differentiate childhood depression. It is understandable that we might presume children should be happy and carefree and have no need to be depressed. The fact remains, however, that children do suffer from depression and sometimes surprise us by taking their life when they appear to be well-adjusted, normal kids.

The *Diagnostic and Statistical Manual* (DSM-IV) criteria reveal similar criteria measures to adult depression; however, as children are moving through different developmental phases, the symptoms may alter so rapidly that they may elude the parent as well as the clinician. Depression in children has a high comorbidity with other conditions such as attention deficit disorder and its resulting social issues such as lack of friends and problematic behavior (Barkley 1988). Obvious risk factors include parental psychopathology, abuse and neglect, sickness and hospitalization or handicapping conditions. Acting-out symptoms frequently become an integral part of the behavior which may act as a "mask" to the symptoms (McKnew, Cytryn and Yahrals 1983). Instead of moping around the house, children translate their concerns into a high-level action or aggressiveness as a defense mechanism. The defense mechanisms are not yet adequately developed to cope with the problems and extreme behavior in either direction should be suspect. Substance abuse is a particular liability. A behavioral approach is the general treatment modality with young children; and yes, they can also benefit from the qigong exercise.

Different diagnostic types of depression

You should not attempt a self diagnosis in an effort to replace professional treatment. Depression is a serious illness and if left untreated, or unmanaged, serious consequences can result. Monitoring for suicidal ideation and behavior is a standard protocol of any treatment plan.

Adjustment disorder with depressed mood

The mildest form of depression and a likely diagnosis when depressive symptoms manifest in response to some specific situational stressor is adjustment disorder with depressed mood. The symptoms appear within three months of the incident and resolve within six months. The individual is markedly distressed and there is impairment in their functioning in the three areas of social interaction, work or intimacy. It would not include bereavement of a loved one. Qigong could be an appropriate treatment application, along with strengthening the support structure and coping mechanisms of the individual.

Seasonal affective disorder (SAD)

If you live in the northern hemisphere and experience depressive symptoms in the autumn or winter, which remit in the spring and summer, and the symptoms are not related to any other issues, SAD could be the problem. Changes in the length of daylight hours can affect our mood, and the best treatment would be to use a natural spectrum light during the winter months. They are readily available, cost-efficient and should be used for about an hour a day to counter the effects of SAD. Qigong could also be beneficial.

Dysthymia

Dysthymia is a chronic depression which comes and goes over a two-year period. It does not exclude the possibility of an incidence of major clinical depression, and it is usually seen in the clinical setting with unresolved personal relationship issues, or accompanied by depressive personality disorder. Daily qigong is highly recommended, as well as insight into the situations which are responsible for creating the fluctuations of mood. The individual often feels powerless and a victim to the circumstances, perhaps displaying an attitude of a martyr.

Major depressive disorder

Major depressive disorder is a clinical unipolar depression. The individual will exhibit a number of the depressive symptoms either in a single episode or as a recurrent experience. The depressed mood and loss of interest in pleasure persists; it cannot be shaken off without intervention. Thoughts of self harm are generally present and medication is usually required, along with talk therapy. Qigong could be practiced daily and consistently.

Family history of depression should be examined. If bipolar genetics are suspected, caution with prescribing medication should be taken. A prescribed antidepressant by a general practitioner who is unaware of a bipolar history may spike the system into the manic phase. Evaluation and appropriate diagnosis should be made by a psychologist or psychiatrist before prescribing medication. Monitoring for suicidal ideation is always recommended.

Bipolar disorder

There is a spectrum of severity and symptom manifestation in a diagnosis of bipolar disorder and it is recognized as having its basis in chemical changes in the brain. Genetic factors are likely present.

Bipolar I disorder is the most severe form which includes symptoms of hyperactivity, irritability, paranoia, grandiosity – such as spending sprees – and deep depression which *may* manifest psychoses. A manic episode must occur to make this diagnosis. Medication is required but the patient is often non-compliant because the high end of the symptoms of the disease is diminished. Depending upon the severity, initial hospitalization may be required to stabilize the patient.

Medication is a lifelong requirement and supportive therapy is necessary to help the patient make lifestyle adjustment and acceptance to this disorder. Family counseling is also suggested to get everyone on board with the treatment plan. Three participants in the qigong clinical research study had the bipolar diagnosis classification, and all three improved their symptoms by using qigong.

Bipolar II disorder is often misdiagnosed because it is characterized by periods of major depression with episodes of hypomania. This is an elevated, euphoric or irritable mood which lasts at least four days. The patient does not exhibit bizarre behavior and the level of impairment is not as severe as a manic episode. It does not usually require hospitalization, and the person's good feelings are commonly seen as a recovery. No psychotic features are present. Medication is required, but again, like Bipolar I, patients are reluctant to give up the only good feelings they have experienced in the hypomanic state. When diagnosing and treating bipolar depression, the only true confirmation of the diagnosis is when the medication works to stabilize the mood. Consequently, there may be a period of time when the medication is adjusted and some chaos and discomfort persists. This is why hospitalization may be necessary until stabilization exists.

There are variations in the frequency of the mood cycling in the bipolar diagnosis. Rapid cycling can often be viewed as a personality disorder because no distinct pattern is readily observable. The individual simply presents as chaotic and emotionally unstable.

Cyclothymic disorder

In cyclothymic disorder, the person experiences frequent mixed mood of hypomania and depression. The swings are not as big up or down, but may manifest a major depressive episode. There may be periods in between where there are no symptoms and a normal mood is present. This is a milder form of bipolar disorder, and many who suffer from this disorder are never seen in the treatment setting. They may self medicate with alcohol or marijuana and are at risk for increase in symptom severity from medication such as decongestants. They may function well, while those who are close to them have adjusted to their mood swings.

Once again, the diagnosis of a mood disorder requires professional evaluation. The material presented in this chapter is provided as psychoeducational and meant to provide information to the individual or family members who can be confused or challenged by how to cope with the illness. There are numerous support groups for both the patient and family members of those who suffer from depression.

Radical acceptance

Shame and denial are major obstacles to effectively dealing with depression. If you had diabetes or high blood pressure, you might look upon it as a medical problem to be dealt with by diet and/or medication. If you can think about depression in this way, it would be helpful. Major depression affects approximately 5–8 percent of the adult population in a given year. If you can accept the illness as a disturbance in the body much as diabetes, this would be a major step toward managing the symptoms. No one wants to deal with the stigma of a mental illness, but unless you accept the fact that mood is affecting your functioning, you are not likely to do anything about it. Once you have identified and accepted the diagnosis and understand the problem, the solution becomes evident and you are likely to experience a sense of joy and hopefulness. At the very least, be grateful for finally understanding the issues which create suffering in your life.

When you face the reality that it is a chemical and energy imbalance in the body that is affecting your spirit, you will understand that it requires your attention, focus and action. You cannot ignore feelings or emotions. These feelings and emotions translate into the information of the neurological system. Do not think of them as failings or annoyances. Embrace your feelings, even those of sadness, as a confirmation of being alive. If I am seeing someone who doesn't feel, someone who cannot identify how they feel, then this is a true tragedy and a major challenge in the therapy setting.

If you have contemplated taking your life as a means to escape the pain of being alive, I would tell you that your existence is precious to the world as a whole and to others. Your perception is misguided, and it is being affected by the imbalance of your neurochemicals system. You may not see this at times of extreme negativity, and I would argue that we all feel inconsequential at times. Value yourself as you might value others; we are all connected in countless ways and your energy is vital to the whole. I agree with the premise that it is hard to live in this world. But I also believe that everyone is doing the very best they can with what information and tools they possess. It is my earnest effort here to provide you with additional tools and knowledge to transcend your needless suffering. The practice of qigong is a valuable tool which you can use to maintain a balance in your mind-body and my research is my gift to you.

Chapter 5

Practical Applications of Qigong to Depression: The Action Plan

If you are suffering from clinical depression, you may want to try qigong as a remedy. Qigong is not meant to replace orthodox medical treatment, but it is a reliable and tested form of complementary and alternative treatment, as you will see from the results in the research study.

There are many individuals who suffer from depression who may be motivated by and attracted to a form of treatment which is natural and non-pharmaceutical. For instance, there are some occupations, such as air traffic controllers, which do not allow for the use of medications. The side effects of antidepressants, such as those affecting sexual drive, may be objectionable to some individuals. Reliance upon external sources for a sense of well-being dooms the individual to dependency, and pharmaceuticals have many side effects.

If you can cultivate, store and manipulate your own energy, this is essentially activating the system of the physical organism at a more fundamental level than mere symptomatic relief. You can learn to mobilize innate healing potential as well as reverse the negative symptoms of depression from your daily life. Personal responsibility for health is taken, and a sense of mastery and self efficacy will result, as well as movement toward the goal of a true state of health, beyond the mere absence of disease. Qigong treatment techniques are a low-tech and cost-effective treatment for depressive disorders as well as anxiety, and directly within the application control of the individual.

Getting started with internal qigong

Master Chunyi Lin has been gracious in allowing the Spring Forest Qigong techniques from his manual to be included in this book, where you will find them in the Appendices (Lin 2000). If you have not yet looked at them, do so now. It is important that you find one of the techniques which you are comfortable with and use it for your daily practice. Daily practice should be at least a 30- or 40-minute period of time, and it is helpful if it is consistent, or at the same time each day. The techniques do not work with a "cafeteria" approach. You will not see success if you do it once in a while or on occasion. Choose one of the exercises you are comfortable doing and make it a routine part of your day.

The task at hand is to build your energy or qi internally through the qigong techniques presented in this book. Daily and regular practice is required to sustain any gains that you might achieve, especially since you may be prone to depleting the energy through old patterns of self neglect or negativity.

Spiritual healing

Depression is an illness of the body and spirit. Qigong has a spiritual element, in that we are drawing on a source of energy beyond the individual. Again, you need not attribute any particular faith or belief system to this technique; and whatever religion you practice need not bias your ability to recover. You can view the energy as God-given or simply from the mechanical universe. If you are a Christian, you may see the energy as Christ's healing power. If you are Jewish, it may come directly from God. If you are Buddhist, you may see it as the healing serenity of Buddha and all that exists. If you have objection to this, visualize it as the healing energy of someone who was kind to you; you may see it as the healing energy of Master Chunyi Lin. The energy is not discriminatory and it is not partial to a particular belief system. You only need to believe and have faith that it is there in abundance and readily available.

Connection with the source

Before undertaking any of the exercises or techniques, use the affirmation or password to set your intent to tap into the source:

I am in the universe. The universe is in my body. The universe and I combine together.

See yourself as connected with the universe and part of the whole of existence. You can see yourself as a speck in the universe, as a droplet of moisture in the sea, or simply a part of the flow of society. You are connected to all things, and in spite of whatever disruption may be happening in your small part of the whole, there is harmony in the existence of the vast universe. See yourself as part of the unified harmony, rather than the discord. In the past, you have been very good at separating yourself from others; use this as an opportunity to relax judgment and experience healing. Allow yourself to see all that is good in yourself and the world.

Deep breathing with intent

The basis of the internal qigong techniques is intent and deep respiratory breathing. Through a combination of mental concentration, breathing techniques and intentional visualization of moving the energy through the body, you will pump up or recharge the energy system. Remember, this technique was developed to increase and conserve energy by the ancient people of China and it has been working for thousands of years to provide healing. Internal qigong is important as the basis or fundamental practice because your internal organs function to support life. As the balance of energy comes back into the body, healing occurs and your health and mood will improve. Deep breathing alone will not heal your body. It is important to look at all the aspects of your life which are creating difficulties, which is why I have discussed depression at length and also included a comprehensive treatment plan in this chapter.

You cannot do the qigong practice while thinking about making dinner or doing something else. You can be doing something like walking or sitting in a vehicle in traffic, but your focus needs to be on the influx of the energy, and the movement of that energy. It is a meditative technique, so it is best done when you can dedicate the time to it. If you lose your concentration, as will happen on occasion, just go back to the breathing and the intent. Relax as much as you can, with your hands and fingers open. Master Lin recommends that your tongue should be touching the roof of your mouth to keep the energy connection. So you should not be talking. Relaxation is an art, and you need to become good at it. Use your mind consciousness to move the energy through the body.

The deep breathing technique is meant to bring oxygen to the body and nervous system. Shallow breathing is anxious breathing and intensifies anxiety; it depletes the nervous system. Focus on your breath and don't force the breathing, just go into a natural, deep, slow breathing pattern. As you continue to practice, you will get better at it, and before long it will become a normal part of your routine physical manner. Remember, we are rewiring the brain and the information system and it will take time.

Adding visualization

If you desire, you can visualize the energy as light, moving into every cell of the body when it enters. This may enhance your practice. When doing the Self Concentration exercise, on the inhalation, I visualize light entering into every pore, cleansing the cells, and when I exhale, I visualize gray smoke exiting the body. My intent is to remove negativity and illness from the body. When I do the Small Universe technique, I am seeing the healing energy of the universe entering my body at a specific point on inhalation, and when I exhale, it moves to the next point. The energy moves in a circular pattern in the torso, down the front, and up the back, as fully explained and demonstrated in the Spring Forest Manual found in the Appendices.

Doing the Small Universe exercise and Self Concentration exercise together, or back-to-back, is very powerful. After doing the exercise several times over several days, you will experience an uplifted sense of spirit and thinking. The longer you practice over time, the more you will increase energy and your ability to maintain the energy. This is important so that when something "wicked" comes along to disturb your equilibrium you will be able to deal with it in a stable, firm manner.

The lower dantian is at the navel. It is emphasized as a core or root of the tree of life (Cohen 1997).

Scientists observe the anatomical features of the fetus to form at different rates and locales, but each organizes interdependently, linked to one another via the connective tissue that still remains as an interlocking web. This web begins and ends at the navel. (Post and Cavaliere 2003, p.52)

A specialized form of qigong called Chi Nei Tsang is dedicated to releasing emotion stored in the stomach. Energy is said to be stored here as in a reservoir. When practicing qigong, you will always bring the energy back to the lower dantian at the termination of practice after the harvest of the qi. The internal qigong practices will open the channels of your torso where the organs are located, which are also considered to be reservoirs of energy. The intentional movement of energy within the torso will increase the flow of energy and healing in the body. It will bring you back into balance after a disturbing event, it will help you fall asleep when you feel you are too keyed up to rest, and you will obtain a more restorative sleep. When done consistently, you are strengthening your physical energy with the practice of internal qigong.

Active Exercise practice

The Active Spring Forest Qigong Exercise is a very effective combination of many complex qigong techniques used for general health.

Master Chunyi Lin has simplified the exercise to include the Small Universe technique of awakening the energy in the torso, opening blockages to heal and balance the energy, and harvesting the energy to store it in reserve. It is a simple technique of eight movements which are repeated for a short period of time – 40 minutes on the DVD. Once you learn the technique, you can do it from memory any time and anywhere. The stronger your focus and intention, the easier you will find the technique and the greater your capacity will be for generating the energy. Once while waiting in an airport, I saw a woman standing off to the side doing the exercise movements before getting on the plane. I immediately recognized the Spring Forest technique, and thought, "What a great way to relieve anxiety and move the energy before a long plane ride."

Your movement should be graceful and generate adequate action to obtain a full range of motion. The action should not be limp or haphazard, or too fast. This will not be the case if you are using the DVD, since it is demonstrated for you with music and you can move along with each exercise. The Active Exercise incorporates a version of Small Universe to begin, and your visualization should be the energy moving in a similar pattern while you are moving your hands in front of you, in the same manner that the energy would be moving in the torso – down the front, and up the back.

The Active Exercise is not strenuous or exertive. I have used the exercise with seniors who were sitting in chairs. Before long, the energy increased and the ability to stand and do the exercise was possible.

Remember, the energy moves with intent and focus, much like biofeedback. The Active Exercise allows you to develop your skill in working with qi and it will create a mind shift in your consciousness. You will be practicing your breathing and be able to allow the body to relax and heal itself. The Active Exercise is a great way to start your day.

External qigong

The research study utilized the qigong masters' emitted qi or wai qi as part of the treatment in each of the subjects. As we have seen earlier, the ability to transfer qi or energy has been shown to exist. The results of the study did show that some of the subjects who were treated by Chunyi Lin himself had greater improvement in somatic (physical) symptoms, but overall the depressive symptoms of all subjects were more readily reduced by their length of practice and consistency of practice. You need not find a qigong master to administer a treatment if one is not available in your area. Some people have asked if a Reiki practitioner will sufficiently suffice. Reiki is not the same discipline and involves the practitioner applying touch, much as in a healing laying-on-of-the-hands application. However, if you feel that you receive benefit from Reiki treatments, then by all means you can supplement your practice with occasional treatments.

When I was teaching a qigong class at a county health department, a member of the class asked me to do some work on her shoulder. I obliged. The pain was relieved and, of course, I was both pleased and surprised. The Spring Forest Qigong exercises for general health are considered to be a Level I practice to maintain general health. With continued effort and practice, a Level II is offered for the development of the ability to transmit qi to heal another. I have worked with Level II to some degree, but my business practice keeps me busy and I use qigong to replenish my own batteries, which become depleted from tending to others in the therapy sessions. I do believe that you can build your qi and energy over time to develop this healing skill; however, it takes a concerted effort and dedication. In session, I utilize the healing intent and focus which I direct toward a patient, and I sincerely believe it makes a difference in the therapeutic setting.

Qigong Institute guidelines

In view of the fact that there is no recognized certificate or licensing system for qigong healers or qigong masters, even in China, the Qigong Institute (1995) has developed the following guidelines to help research scientists who are interested in qigong research to select the appropriate qigong healers or masters in their scientific exploration of qigong.

In general, a good qigong healer or master should meet *at least three* of the following criteria:

1. A specially invited member or director of the Chinese Society of Qigong Science (over a thousand of such members existing in China who have been officially evaluated by the Society).

2. A recorded history of scientific research (with published papers or certified reports).

3. A member of the national or international professional qigong organizations.

4. A formal disciple of the traceable and renowned qigong master or qigong tradition, such as lineage holder or representative of a special form.

5. A solid medical training or background, and preferably belonging to some kind of national organization of medical practitioners.

6. An individual who does not currently have any verifiable negative claim against him/her in the field.

7. An individual who has an established qigong healing practice in their country of residence or a visitor who has similar qualifications in their home country.

The three qigong masters who participated in my study met the standards above, and I would suggest that, when you search out a practitioner, you ask them about their training and techniques.

A treatment plan for depression using qigong as an alternative and complementary technique

When I am working with a client, I will always provide them with a copy of the treatment plan, and ask them to sign a copy of it. We both need to be on the same page with our goals and expectations. I always go over the assessment data and provide evaluation feedback to them. I make the clients aware of the diagnosis, and give them an estimate of how long I expect to be working with them. This is good standard practice, and I am sometimes surprised when other therapists choose not to do this. Consequently, I am providing a generic treatment plan for depression as an example. If you are working with a therapist, it may help you to have some knowledge about the process, and if you are not, it will provide a guideline for your work toward wellness.

The treatment plan for depression comprises both immediate methods and long-term therapeutic interventions.

Immediate methods to ameliorate the current state of clinical depressive symptoms

There are five immediate methods to consider.

1. *Assess the symptoms and evaluate the need for medication and safety*

   A suicide risk assessment may be appropriate. Does this individual have thoughts of killing themselves, or persistent thoughts about dying? Is there a plan to carry out the action? Is there a history of suicide attempts? Is there poor impulse control, substance abuse, or a poor support system? Has the individual experienced a recent loss? Do not assume that because a person is talking about dying that they won't do it. Is medication an appropriate recommendation?

2. *Advocate cognitive behavioral therapy (CBT)*

   Goal: Improve problem solving and coping.

Identify the problem and dysfunctional coping. Identify mistaken beliefs and negative misperceptions. Counter the pessimistic expectations and self deprecation. Diminish the hopelessness and pain which the individual is experiencing through reframing the problem and identify plausible solutions. Work toward an understanding about the condition of being overwhelmed and break the situation down into manageable chunks. Encourage self focus and self care. Facilitate clarification of boundaries as it relates to others. Provide positive feedback for decision-making and movement toward appropriate goals. Decrease symptomology through education about depression. Utilize thought stopping for negativity and reframe with a strength-based, positive outlook.

3. *Develop resources and support structure*
Goal: Identify and utilize resources and support systems which may have been previously avoided.
Moderate the hypersensitivity, anxiety and anticipation of rejection. Convey acceptance and positive regard to create a safe and non-judgmental environment. Identify events and individuals in your life which have been positive and encouraging. Resist the desire to withdraw and isolate. Make an effort to have social contact with others every day. Learn to use assertive-style communication to get your needs met. Seek alternative responses and solutions for dealing with stressful situations. Use appropriate risk-taking in attempting new behaviors and challenge yourself. Practice daily qigong to build energy and enhance balance of neurological system. See the unlimited resource of the universe at your availability.

4. *Build self esteem*
Goal: Revive the sense of self worth and promote optimistic cognitive shifts.
Focus on your strengths and accomplishments. Do not dwell on your past, nor be anxious about the future. Take care of just today. Reframe negative events to create an

understanding and learning ability from them. Do something for yourself each day that provides you with some small sense of pleasure, even if it is just taking a walk. Accept responsibility for your thinking and mental health. Identify what you want to change about your life and establish realistic objectives to meet the challenge. Use your support structure to help you attain them. Use relaxation techniques such as muscle relaxation, deep breathing and visualization to see yourself as healthy and whole. Visualize yourself accomplishing your goals. Use daily qigong to see the self as connected to others and balance energy patterns. Focus on positive self talk and thoughts.

5. *Improve sleep disturbances*
   Goal: To improve physical, neurological balance and health.
   Evaluate diet for sugar and caffeine intake. Drink an appropriate amount of water to hydrate. Eliminate daytime naps, and utilize exercise such as walking. Routinely do a daily 40-minute qigong practice, preferably the Active Exercise. Refrain from watching television in the bedroom. Have a routine schedule for bedtime which might include a hot bath and down-time before sleep. Eliminate stressful conversation before bed. Have a light snack, such as turkey with cottage cheese. Learn to let go of the day with a brief meditation to clear the mind. Use the Small Universe exercise while lying in bed. Use an affirmation that "I will now have a deep and restorative sleep and awaken refreshed and content in the morning."

Long-term therapeutic interventions

Long-term therapeutic interventions should be considered once the more pressing and acute difficulties are diminished. The following six interventions will serve to prevent a reoccurrence of the problems.

1. *Continue to monitor for the need of medication or compliance,* as well as thoughts of self harm.

2. *Establish appropriate goals for personal growth and behavior change.* This may include psychotherapy, reading self help books or practicing insight meditation.

3. *Recognize character traits which may have led to the depression.* Make efforts to identify the mistaken beliefs and patterns. Work toward changing them with realistic goals. For example, perfectionism and controlling tendencies can be changed to acceptance of self and others with flaws. Extend love to yourself. Learn the virtues of acceptance and forgiveness.

4. *Accomplish ego-strengthening* by making small challenges to yourself and then following through with a plan toward completion. Stretch and move beyond your comfort zone. Remember your strengths and past accomplishments. Using the discipline of qigong will help you to gain a calmer and more resolute attitude and to move energy patterns more successfully.

5. *Practice good boundaries with your self and others* to reduce stress and to enhance your ability to maintain healthy personal relationships. Refrain from black-and-white thinking, judgment of others or holding them on a pedestal. Remember the goal of acceptance. Learn to be grateful and to acknowledge how far you have come.

6. *Practice daily qigong.* If you are feeling better, you will want to maintain the energy flow and healthy state. Do not allow yourself to become depleted again. Maintenance of the practice and the system health is an important part of the change model.

· *Chapter 6* ·

Taking Personal
Responsibility
for Your Health

The Spring Forest Qigong technique is simple to do and it is not costly for the individual to maintain. The cost of antidepressant medication can be high and residual side effects are often experienced.

In the USA, the cost of health care takes a significant percentage of the family budget, and medical spending has risen 2 percent faster annually than the rest of the economy. All developed countries have experienced medical inflation, and there is a marginal impact on cost control despite the differently structured national health systems. The health care system is burdened by the expectation that it can provide health through the remedy of medicine. The current accepted mode of treatment for depression, the most commonly diagnosed mental difficulty, includes cognitive behavioral therapy and medication. I hope that this research will make an impact upon how depression is treated as well as how it is viewed by others.

The perspective that we are interconnected through an energy field and that this energy can be exchanged in human interactions, whether they be through thoughts, emotions or physical action, is a major shift in the scientific paradigm which is not addressed in the current accepted therapies. An energetic approach to depression offers the opportunity to change our perception about human relationships and how to modulate our own response to "toxic environments" and their effects upon our own energy field. The subjects in this research study were not removed from their everyday difficulties, nor were they given psychotherapy; they were trained in how to better cope with and balance their emotional world and to develop a sense of self mastery. A balanced control of their response was the goal, rather than a dependency upon medication or the need to see a therapist. You cannot put a value on such a tool; it is priceless.

The research subjects learned to mobilize their innate healing potential and reverse the negative effects of depression in the curative sense. This is the first study to apply qigong as a curative in depression. The technique is not a short-term, temporary measure, but offers a lifetime modality for dealing with stress, genetic vulnerability, and the negative effects of depression. The technique is cost-effective and there were no reported side effects of the exercise when done as instructed.

The results provided a significant improvement in all subjects. In applications of a new treatment, only a few events of sufficiently high significance can be enough to assert that a new phenomenon exists with a high level of confidence; this study indicates a very significant level of improvement in the majority of the subjects who were measured at serious and debilitating levels of depression. Their lives improved over a short period of time and they became self sufficient in their ability to manage the symptoms which they suffered from.

A decrease of energy is a common factor of depression and there are complex factors involved. Normal mood changes of anxiety, disappointment and sadness may be an incipient factor in shutting down or closing of the solar plexus chakra, or the lower dantian, which is said to be responsible for the main energy flow intake. As the whole system is energetically recharging at a lower rate, the individual is expending more energy through dealing with turbulent feelings, and consequently less energy is available. Anxious and depressed individuals tend to breathe in a shallow pattern, and this will also affect the flow of oxygen and energy into the body. The qigong exercise encourages a deep and measured breath. It is common to see most depressed patients slumped over, almost as if protecting the area of the solar plexus, the reputed source of intake for vital energy.

As the individual becomes more self involved, thinking about his or her problems, the mental field closes inward on the negative self, less and less energy is exchanged and the chakra may become more and more blocked. Ultimately, as the situation does not improve, the individual reaches a stage where any activity becomes a major undertaking and the illness becomes a part of the accepted identity. The resulting lack of self confidence creates feelings of guilt and reduces energy even further. As the individual isolates, becoming even more self centered, the ability to change the circumstances or themselves is further reduced. The thought patterns affect the neuropeptides and the information system. But they also affect the energy system – which we have seen – which perhaps is a precursor to the neurochemistry.

The dorsal portals of the chakras are believed to affect the will and conscious choice (Brennan 1988). The will becomes blocked in depression because one gets locked into one's own feelings and thoughts, closing down those energy transformers. Consequently, it is too hard to change or find a way out, although there may be a desire to change. To mobilize the will requires energy, and when energy is outwardly directed, it enables the individual to relate to others, which again enhances the energy field. By directing one's will to go outward and tap the vast and abundant source, the depressed person whose previous focus was mainly on self is able to initiate the thrust toward health.

This model extends beyond the cognitive behaviorist's model of depression in which either internal or external conditioned stimuli trigger the conditioned depressive response. The theory is reflective of Adlerian theories of social interest and the importance of maintaining a conscious connection with the whole. The qigong exercise specifically uses visualization of a connection with a unified conciousness and drawing upon that energy, actually reaching up and out to the cosmos. This dynamic movement and symbolism alone is an important avenue toward improvement in reaching out to others as well as the source.

The process of relaxation increases the flow of this energy through the solar plexus chakra, increasing reserves of vital energy. It does not matter whether you call it biofeedback or qigong; what is required is the conscious choice to draw upon the force: it is the *intent* that makes the difference. This is the basic premise in qigong. The practitioners' clearing of blockages may have been instrumental to some of the subjects; however, what was more important was the mobilization of will and a redirection of the focus of emotional and intellectual energy from withdrawing and shrinking to outgoing-ness and drawing upon the resources of the universe. The signifi-cance was not due to individual practitioners, or even whether they received a real or sham qi emission treatment, it was based upon a consistent use of the exercise and the belief that this resource was available to them.

There was a major reframing of the perception of the present and future, from the absence of hope to the possibility of a potent and unlimited resource, within the complete control of the subject. The reality is that qigong made each subject feel extraordinarily better in a short period of time; qi and its healing potential was real for them and did not require any further explanation. The reduc-tion of symptoms, feeling better and getting back into active life was the true measure as far as the participants were concerned.

Qigong as a basic health care preventative

The price of being well should not be limited by funding, access to care or rationing schemes of cost containment, no matter where you live. These schemes do not affect the real factors which are respon-sible for spiraling health care costs: population growth of elderly people, rising hospital or care home costs, and technological inno-vation. When I worked in the insurance industry between 1969 and 1995, I witnessed and tried to control for abuse of the system on both ends – the providers and the insured. While a medical claim can be paid in two days, it is wise to remember that insurance companies are essentially investment companies. A company will delay or deny payment because it is in their best interest. As investments go, the risk in covering health liability is not a great one. Many insurance carriers have removed themselves from the marketplace for this very reason. The system is broken, and we know it. The ultimate solution is within each individual.

There is a need for a broadened concept of health in our society that emphasizes individual responsibility. Unfortunately, a large segment of the population has relinquished its rights to accountability for health, and as a result there has been a general loss of control by the individual over the goals and direction of the health care system. A passive patient relieved of responsibility allows modern medicine and technology to solve his problems, encouraging others to do for us and to us. We have a narrow conception of "health" to mean the absence of disease. A broadened definition of factors such as wellness, environmental health and lifestyle needs to be included. The recent paradigm shift toward holistic health measures which include energy applications such as qigong can be viewed as an encouraging sign. The ultimate answer is wellness with individual responsibility for the maintenance of same. The qigong exercise gives the individual the power to create balance within the physical body and offers a better opportunity to maintain health.

Everyone is different, and each person has individual ideals and values. "Different strokes for different folks" has become the means to acceptance of different cultures and just plain getting along with others. There is no shared-value system in our pluralistic society with the one exception of health. Even freedom is not to be enjoyed without the prospect of health. Health as it relates to the values and meaning of a full life is a part of each individual's private life. Some are more diligent about maintaining their health than others, but all would agree that good health is necessary to well-being. Health has slowly become the supreme value and one which possesses a quasi-religious quality and sometimes serves to replace the more complex question of the meaning of life. Ethical issues of survival often are addressed to the quality of life. As humans, struggling with the issues of life, we are all connected and similar. The universal resource tapped by qigong makes no differentiation between cultures or class.

The concept of preventative intervention is strongly related to an individual's way of life. Illness is personalized and we tend to make maintenance of health a moral obligation. Many are accused of living the "wrong lifestyle" or told to "change their lifestyle" which interferes with our rights, as in the case of a smoker's rights. There is great debate today about the rights of individuals and little about taking ownership for health. Health care may be viewed as a basic negative right, or claim, suggesting that others may not interfere with or must refrain from actions that threaten health. As a positive right, the government must take steps to improve conditions that threaten health. Based on principles of distributive justice, smokers, alcoholics and high-risk individuals may have increased needs. In evaluating the goals of a health system, the complex issues of different objectives can be considered, but the basic desire is health and freedom to enjoy life. It is puzzling to consider why anyone would put that control into the hands of others.

There are limits to government and societal authority and, even where health care is nationalized, black markets can arise to supplement programs. Even in countries with socialized medicine, many have supplemental health care plans. The answer and real control lies within each individual to take responsibility for their own health, and the daily practice of qigong can be instrumental to that end.

The four goals in health care cannot be achieved equally, because they are not compatible. These are the best of care, equality of care, cost containment, and optimum choice of provider by the consumer. We must settle for a compromise in our priorities and values in any system proposed. Even with the most advanced medical technology and an abundance of superb specialists and hospitals on an international scale, we cannot expect miracles to rescue us. The soaring cost of care threatens to deny even affluent individuals access to the ideals of health which we have come to expect.

The time is right to take responsibility for your own health and to stop reliance upon the system. Millions of people do not have access to good medical care and many do not understand the impact of toxic emotions upon health.

I challenge you to take control of this one aspect of your life, which is a key to your sense of well-being. There is strong evidence that a correlation exists between emotional and physical illness. The substantial evidence that stressors are related to the course of depression, and that indeed qigong does make a difference in how the body responds to these stressors, is now a part of your own knowledge. The question is, what will you now do with it?

By the practice of qigong, you may begin the path to be free of suffering. Happiness is an illusive and temporary state; but you now have one tool to find peace and contentment in your life. I trust you will use it and encourage others to do so as well.

· *Chapter 7* ·

The Clinical
Research Study

The fact that qigong has been shown to increase serotonin levels was the main motivator for my interest in the study. At the time I undertook the proposal for the study, I had been a meditator for over 30 years and had experienced the benefits of a calm and peaceful acceptance of events in my life. I understood the effects of meditation on the mind-body and I was intrigued by the addition of movement. I had done a walking meditation in retreat previously, and qigong was much easier than tai chi, which I had attempted.

Finding three professors in a fairly conservative academic environment who were willing to sponsor my dissertation work took caution even in approaching them with the subject of qigong. One of the psychologists at my internship made facetious remarks to me about bending spoons when I began recruiting subjects for the study from the clinical population. This was a pioneer venture and most topics of dissertation are safe subjects, perhaps reanalyzing some aspect of another theory. In many ways, I was out on a limb with this topic; but because this was a second career for me, I was not as dependent upon the approval of the old guard. I felt the risk was worth it.

This chapter will explain how the research experiment was conducted in simple terms, and for those readers in the psychology field, statistical data are provided.

Methodology

I interviewed 72 subjects either in person or on the telephone. Volunteers were recruited through newspaper advertisement, flyers in the western suburbs of the Chicago area and the clinical population of Kendall County, where I was doing an internship. The subjects were screened for situational depression, schizophrenia, psychosis and dissociative experiences; 63 subjects were initially accepted into the study based upon the DSM-IV criteria for major clinical depression. Several then dropped out because of time commitments or they couldn't meet the minimum requirements of the study. The final sample was therefore composed of 39 volunteers; all subjects were adults (18+) and ranged in age between 23 and 69 years, with a mean of age 50. Female gender was predominant, which was to be expected due to their prevalence in reporting depression and seeking help. There were 34 women and 5 men. Subjects met the criteria of DSM-IV diagnosis of a depressive mood disorder, specifically dysthymia or major depression. There were three subjects who met criteria for bipolar disorder who were medication compliant and approved to participate in the study – yet another hurdle in the approval process. These subjects were screened to exclude psychoticism and paranoid features.

The study did not exclude individuals who were currently taking medication and, of the 39 individuals, 18 reported taking an antidepressant medication. There were numerous individuals with reported health difficulties, including one man who had a brain tumor.

The participants were divided into three groups and assigned to an individual qi master practitioner. Subjects were given name tags, some of which were all upper-case letters and some of which were both upper- and lower-case letters as a way to identify subgroups.

Instruments used

The three qi masters were selected using the Qigong Institute (1995) *Guidelines for Selecting Qigong Healers in the Scientific Research of*

Qigong. Since 1976 Master Chunyi Lin has studied in China with respected masters in remote regions and practiced austere meditation in caves. He reports the ability to evaluate energy movement by sight as well as sense through the hands. He developed the Spring Forest Qigong technique and has taught qigong to over 30,000 students at the University of St. Thomas, Park Nicollet Medical Center, University of Minnesota, Anoka Ramsey Community College and the University of Toledo. Master Lin's private practice has had, at the time of the study, over 8000 patient visits and he has participated in studies with Hazelden and the University of Minnesota. The former director of the David Hickok Memorial Cancer Research Laboratory acknowledges that the Spring Forest techniques are simple and have added significantly to the quality of life of cancer patients at the clinic. Master Lin has also received a research grant from the Mayo Clinic.

Renee Ryan is on the faculty of the Wellness and Massage Training Institute where she teaches tai chi, qigong and other disciplines. She also teaches qigong at the Theosophical Society in Wheaton, Illinois. She has practiced the healing arts since the mid-1980s and has studied qigong in the United States, China and Korea. She currently maintains a practice in Winfield, Illinois.

Jim Nance is a student of Master Chunyi Lin and the Spring Forest technique. He has worked with Master Lin since 1995, both practicing and teaching qigong on a full-time basis. He has a degree in education and became interested in qigong as a result of his martial arts background. Master Lin has certified him at the highest level of certification for Qi Master. He is believed to be the first African American in history to obtain the qualification.

The Beck's Depression Inventory–Revised (BDI-R) and the Symptom Checklist-90 (SCL-90) were used to measure clinical symptoms. The BDI-R investigates six of the nine criteria of the DSM diagnosis for depression, and gender correlates with BDI scores. The BDI-R has a high rate of internal consistency (0.73 to 0.95) and is a simple self-report instrument which can be done in five to ten minutes. The SCL-90 provides a Likert scale for self-report data on a wide range of items – 90 of them – which are indicative of psychological distress. These indices cover anxiety, depression, interpersonal sensitivity, and others. The SCL-90 is a widely accepted and used instrument and correlates (0.55) with the MCMI-III somatoform scale. The tests were administered before the admittance of the participants at the first meeting to provide a baseline measure, the second meeting a month later, and at the conclusion of the clinical trial, which was a month afterward.

Blood pressure readings were administered by qualified registered nurses. The readings were taken directly before and after the administration of qi, or wai qui, by the qi masters in each group.

The subjects were also evaluated by a self-report supplementary questionnaire to determine a change in conditions during the treatment period: whether they began or discontinued medication; whether their life situation had changed and how; whether they had participated in the qigong exercises; and change in behavior and symptomology. Detailed practice logs were maintained by each subject indicating the length of daily practice in both the dynamic and meditative exercises. Consent forms were signed by all subjects.

Each participant received a videotape of the Spring Forest Qigong exercise (40 minutes) as well as two audiotapes which included the dynamic exercise and meditative exercises (30 minutes each). The written manual was also provided.

Procedures followed

The subjects met three times, over a two-month period. At the first meeting, Master Lin demonstrated and explained the Spring Forest Small Universe exercise. Each qigong master's group was divided into two subgroups and identified by the name tag by upper or lower case, unbeknown to the participants. This procedure was used for the first session only. Each subject met with a qi master for a 10-minute private session. One subgroup received a 10-minute individual session in which a genuine qi emission treatment was given from the master. The other subgroup did not. Subjects who did not receive the genuine qi emission treatment were not aware of the sham treatment. On the second and third meeting, all participants received a genuine 10-minute qi emission treatment.

While giving the sham treatment, the qi masters were instructed to think of something else while administering wai qi.

The subjects were given a pre- and post-treatment blood pressure reading at each meeting. Subjects were instructed to practice daily utilizing the 40-minute videotape and audiotapes. They were also instructed to record the amount of time they practiced on specific daily log sheets which were provided.

At no time were individuals touched by the qigong practitioner. The qigong practitioner utilizes a technique of qi emission which is a non-intrusive transfer of healing subtle energy between the practitioner and the subject. *No subjects were provided counseling or psychotherapy at any time.* The subjects were provided with contact information for the researcher to report problems or if any ill effects occurred from doing the exercise. There were no such occurrences. Only incidental inquiries were received regarding process or to report a feeling of well-being. Five individuals dropped out for reasons of scheduling. Results were reported on a number of different variables.

Research results

All subjects improved during the course of the treatment over the two-month period. See Figure 7.1.

The values of all measured results were statistically analyzed using an Analysis of Variance (ANOVA). The following dependent variables were analyzed separately: on the BDI-R, Depression; and on the SCL-90, the indices of Depression (Dep), Interpersonal Sensitivity (IS) and Somaticism (Som). Interpersonal Sensitivity criteria relate to feeling bad about oneself, and Somaticism specifically targets bodily aches and pains, such as headaches, which are common to those who suffer from depression. Three symptoms from the supplementary questionnaire were also examined by controlling for the variables with Analysis of Covariance (ANCOVA). The effects of these covariates were minimal and negligible.

TEST 1 RESULTS

Assessment Measure	N	Test 1	Min.	Max.	Standard
BD1	39	19.13	1	40	9.74
SCLIS	39	66.51	50	81	8.22
SCL DEP	39	67.97	46	81	8.43
SCL SOM	39	60.15	7	83	12.20
SYM 1	39	1.54	1	3	0.82
SYM 4	39	1.69	1	3	0.80
SYM 5	39	20.5	1	3	0.92

TEST 2 RESULTS

Assessment Measure	N	Test 2	Min.	Max.	Standard
BD1	39	8.69	0	30	7.20
SCLIS	39	53.41	0	81	18.35
SCL DEP	39	53.72	0	81	19.02
SCL SOM	39	49.26	0	45	16.86
SYM 1	39	4.64	1	3	0.87
SYM 4	39	1.82	1	3	0.91
SYM 5	39	1.79	1	3	0.86

TEST 3 RESULTS

Assessment Measure	N	Test 3	Min.	Max.	Standard
BD1	34	7.82	0	31	7.49
SCLIS	34	53.71	39	81	11.13
SCL DEP	34	56.76	34	81	10.88
SCL SOM	34	50.50	35	69	10.46
SYM 1	34	1.18	1	2	0.39
SYM 4	34	1.26	1	3	0.57
SYM 5	34	1.38	1	3	0.74

Figure 7.1 Descriptive statistics

Separate ANOVAs were conducted for each of the following treatment comparisons: (1) exercise time; (2) medication; (3) practitioner; (4) blood pressure; (5) treatment versus non-treatment groups; (6) whether the subject experienced more environmental stress; (7) whether the subject had the belief or expectancy that the exercise was helping; and (8) whether the subject stated they would continue the exercise.

There were no negative effects reported as a result of doing the qigong exercise and there were no reports of deviation syndrome. There was a noticeable difference in the affect and presentation of the subjects between the first and third meeting. The practitioners commented, as well, on their original concern at the first meeting about how "serious" and sad the subjects looked. By the last session, the subjects displayed an enthusiastic attitude and their affect was markedly changed to a more responsive and animated level. They were genuinely curious about the qigong technique and made inquiry about advanced levels of practice.

For purposes of analysis, subjects were considered to be compliant with the exercise requirement if they did 40 minutes of exercise daily (1200 minutes for the month), which was the length of the videotape. This may have included the meditative exercise as well, and although separate data were maintained, no differentiation was made for which technique was used. While there was an overall significant effect over the treatment period, *the strongest gains were made in the first month.* There are strong indicators of consistent improvement over time, or a trend of improvement, and it should be noted that the research indicates larger gains after the first year. The two-month figures are indicative of the building trend.

During the first month of the study, there was significant improvement on both scaled scores of the BDI – a mean of 20 fell to a mean of 9; and on the SCL-90, Depression (Dep), a mean of 69 fell to a mean of 57. BDI: $F (df\ 1,35) = 43.752$; $p = 0.00000$. See Figure 7.2.

The statistical value for proof of significance of a treatment is 0.05, and as you can see from the measure of 0.00000, this value was greatly surpassed. There was little question that the qigong

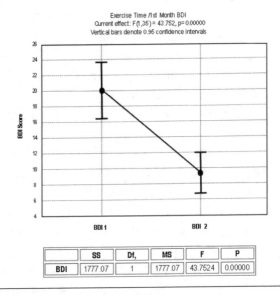

Figure 7.2 The BDI; all subjects reduced their scores to a significant degree (0.00000), well beyond the 0.05 level of significance required to show that the exercise had an effect

exercise had made a difference in the symptoms of depression as reported by subjects on the BDI.

On the SCL-90 Depression was measured as F (df 1,35) = 22.864; p = 0.00003. See Figure 7.3.

Depression improved in the second month at the third measure, but no significant improvement was indicated except on the SCL Dep score with the exercise-compliant group. See Figure 7.4.

The amount of exercise appeared not to be a significant factor for the improvement of the depressive symptoms. What was more important was that it was consistent.

Both groups made a significant improvement on the SCL Interpersonal Sensitivity (IS) score in the first month regardless of exercise time; a mean of 67 dropped to a mean of 57. F (df 1,35) = 23.525; p = 0.00003. See Figure 7.5.

The significant improvement was also observed for the second month with a mean of 58 dropping to a mean of 53. The exercise-compliant group was measured at p = 0.013. Overall, SCL-90 (IS)

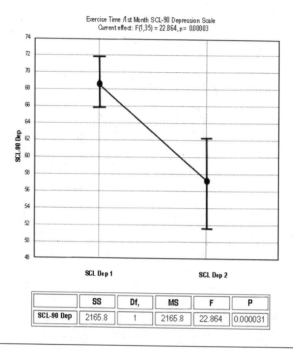

Figure 7.3 The SCL-90; all subjects reduced their depression scores to a significant degree (0.000031)

scores were significantly decreased for the treatment period of two months; the mean fell from 67 to 53.

Overall, SCL Somaticism scores improved significantly from the first to the second month with a mean of 69 to 53 observed – F (df 1,35) = 5.0699; p = 0.03 and also in the second to the third month, with a mean of 55 falling to a mean of 49 – F (df 1,32) = 9.2533; p = 0.0004 – with the exercise-compliant group observed at p = 0.006. Exercise time did not affect the improvement from the first to the second month, but the exercise-complaint group made a very significant improvement from the second to the third month.

When comparing the supplementary scales, symptoms of sleep (Symptom 1) and feeling sad, blue and worthless (Symptom 4), there was no change from the first to the second month with respect to exercise time, but a significant improvement was observed from the second to the third measure, indicating a trend building. The

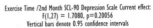

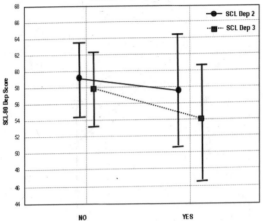

Newman-Keuls test; Probabilities for Post-Hoc Tests
Error; Between: Within; Pooled MS=115.72, df=36.434

	Ex. Compliance	R1	(1)	(2)	(3)	(4)
1	No	SCL Dep 2		0.498704	0.960485	0.578656
2	No	SCL Dep 3	0.498704		0.902500	0.730752
3	Yes	SCL Dep 2	0.960485	0.92500		0.016553
4	Yes	SCL Dep 3	0.578656	0.730752	0.016553	

Figure 7.4 The SCL-90 and exercise compliance; the subjects who were compliant with the exercise requirement (Yes) experienced a greater level of relief in depressive symptoms

overall improvement from the first to the third month was significant (Symptom 1 p = 0.02; Symptom 4 p = 0.01). See Figure 7.6.

Blood pressure reductions were experienced across all groups, even for those who did a low amount of the exercise (less than 500 minutes for the month). F (df 1,27) = 13.344; p = 0.00110. See Figure 7.7.

Medication

The effects of antidepressant medication were reviewed by repeated measure of ANOVA and also controlling for the medication

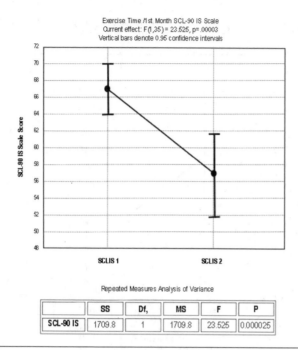

Figure 7.5 The SCL and interpersonal sensitivity; after the first month of the exercise, the subjects' SCL IS scores dropped significantly (0.000025) and their self esteem improved dramatically

and exercise variables with ANCOVA using the BDI and SCL Depression scale. The effect of this covariate was minimal and negligible. Controlling for the exercise time did not change the result. This result indicates *that the medication appeared not to have a significant effect upon the depression over the treatment period.* See Figure 7.8.

Practitioner

Repeated measures of ANOVA were done comparing the different groups by practitioner relative to their results on the various measurements. Overall, there was little difference in the effectiveness of the practitioners. All subjects improved, as was expected, receiving benefit from the daily qigong exercise. It should be noted that Practitioner Renee Ryan's group incidentally had higher baseline

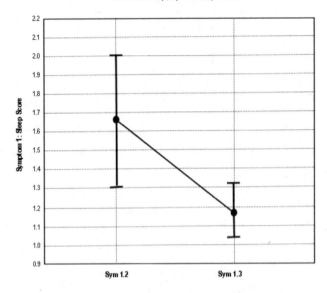

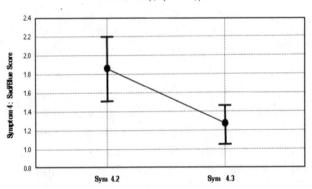

Figure 7.6 Symptoms; (top) subjects reported an improvement in their ability to sleep to a significant degree (0.02315) and {bottom) subjects reported a significant reduction in the depressive symptom "feeling sad and blue" (0.012218)

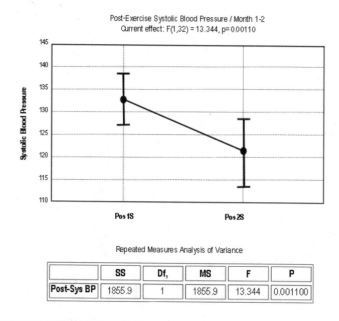

Figure 7.7 Systolic blood pressure; a significant reduction (0.001100) was observed between the first month reading and the measure taken at the second meeting

scores on most of the instruments which were used in measurement than the other two groups. The groups were randomly assigned, before any measurements were taken at the first session, and the name tags were printed assigning the subjects to either a genuine or sham treatment.

The subjects in all groups improved significantly over the course of the treatment period on the BDI, and between practitioners, only Chunyi Lin's group made a more significant improvement on the SCL Somaticism scale for the entire treatment period.

Blood pressure readings at each of the three sessions varied and changes were noted for each of the groups. There were general indications of a drop in blood pressure after the 10-minute treatment session, with some as many as 20 points; however, no overall significance was reported by specific practitioners.

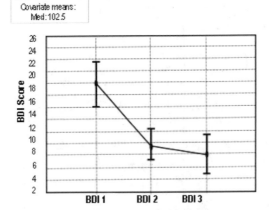

BDI Treatment Period Current effect: F(2, 62) = 2.7237,
p = 0.07349, Covariate: Medication

Covariate means:
Med: 102.5

Repeated Measures Analysis of Variance

	SS	Df,	MS	F	p
Med	87.513	1	87.5133	0.589111	0.448570
BDI	156.527	2	78.2637	2.723745	0.073586
BDI*Med	163.090	3	81.5449	2.837935	0.066175

Newman-Keuls test; variable, Probabilities for Post-Hoc Tests
Error; Between: Within; Pooled MS=70.021, df=57.736, Covariate: Medication

	Exercise Compliance	BDI	{1}	{2}	{3}	{4}	{5}	{6}
1	Yes	BDI 1		0.000116	0.000132	0.150517	0.000287	0.000151
2	Yes	BDI 2	0.000116		0.909074	0.032075	0.875311	0.713320
3	Yes	BDI 3	0.000132	0.909074		0.076163	0.971180	0.593434
4	No	BDI 1	0.150517	0.032075	0.076163		0.001183	0.000165
5	No	BDI 2	0.000287	0.875311	0.971180	0.001183		0.409955
6	No	BDI 3	0.000151	0.713320	0.593434	0.000165	0.409955	

Newman-Keuls test; Probabilities for Post-Hoc Tests: Error: Within MS=29.714, df=64.000

	BDI	{1}	{2}	{3}
1	BDI 1	0	0.000109	0.000116
2	BDI 2	0.000109		0.134773
3	BDI 3	0.000116	0.134773	

Figure 7.8 Medication; when the statistical analysis was adjusted for those who were taking medication, the qigong exercise was found to be more of a factor for improvement on the BDI scores than medication

Treatment and non-treatment groups

ANOVA was done with repeated measures with respect to the treatment and non-treatment groups and their results on the various measures. There was no significant difference found on the BDI and SCL scales, nor the supplementary questions for the treatment period. At the first session, the treatment group (those that received the genuine qi emission) experienced a very significant improvement in the post-systolic reading. F (df 1,37) = 11.755; p = 0.001. There was no significance between treatment groups for the diastolic readings at the first session.

At session two, both subgroups received a qi emission and both experienced a lower reading at both systolic and diastolic measures. There was a significant improvement within the treatment group again for diastolic measured readings (p = 0.03), even though both groups received a qi emission treatment.

Blood pressure systolic readings for the entire group were reduced significantly at the second session (p = 0.001) and the treatment group had a significantly lower systolic reading from the previous month (p = 0.006).

More environmental stress

A subject was attributed with more environmental stress if it was considered to be a major life stressor. Examples are: filing for divorce or separating from spouse; experiencing a family member being hospitalized for psychiatric treatment; having a grandchild move in because the parents are no longer able to care for the child; losing a support system; starting a new job; becoming a caretaker for a nephew with Huntington's disease; and stopping hormone replacement therapy (HRT) as a result of the negative research studies which were published at this time.

ANOVA was done with respect to reported increased levels of stress. *Those subjects who reported more stressors in their life, and continued to do some qigong exercise, continued to experience benefits through the reduction of most symptoms.* There were no significant levels of difference between the comparative groups, and it appeared that the exercise acted as a deterrent to greater depression. There were a few individuals with more stress who did not do the exercise because they felt there was less time for it. In this case, symptoms were reported to be experienced at an increased level.

Belief the exercise was helping

The belief that the qigong exercise would be helpful was an important predictor in the improvement of symptoms and success in treatment. There was significant improvement on the BDI scale for the subjects who reported that the exercise was helpful. F (df 1,32) $= 7.1674; p = 0.01$. This effect was also seen on the other measures of SCL Depression, Somaticism and Interpersonal Sensitivity Scales.

Anecdotal reports

Specific reports of somatic and symptom relief were reported which deserve to be mentioned. First, one woman stated that the ringing in her ear had disappeared immediately after the first qi emission treatment administered by the practitioner. She reported that she had consistently experienced this ringing for a period of nine years. Second, another woman who suffered from diabetes stated that she had reduced her insulin levels. Third, another woman with numerous physical problems stated that she no longer needed to take the prescription pain-reliever Vicodin to sleep at night, and she began a job after a long period of not working. Fourth, another woman stated she had cut her antidepressant medication in half. Fifth, another woman stated that she found she could get answers to her numerous problems while doing the meditative qigong exercise.

Discussion of results

The study was conducted as a preliminary pilot test to determine if qigong could be a useful technique in the treatment of depression.

The study was not designed to measure qi, or to determine what qi is composed of. The reduction in blood pressure after a qi emission treatment was indicative that something occurred or some transference took place between the subject and the practitioner. I was very interested to see if we could measure this phenomenon for reporting, which was why I hired registered nurses to attend each meeting.

The research study results were most successful in that the subjects reported significant and substantial relief of symptoms connected with DSM-IV guidelines for depression and there were no negative side effects of the treatment. The physical presentation and appearance of the group was markedly different and improved at the end of the treatment period than when they first presented two months earlier. It should also be noted that the effects of qigong are long term, and the study treatment period lasted only two months.

All subjects improved; however, the exercise-compliant group had a reported higher level of improvement on Symptom 4 (sad, blue and worthless) than the non-compliant group. The amount of exercise appeared not to be a significant factor; however, a trend of improvement was exhibited, indicating that the qigong exercise appears to have a long-term effect rather than a short-term effect. The greater results are exhibited after the first year of practice, according to the research material (Kawano 1998a; Kawano *et al.* 1997). As improvement was experienced, however, the exercise time decreased. As with any intervention, when the symptoms are relieved, the compliance dissipated. There was a greater improvement by the third measure in the exercise-compliant group. No differentiation was made for active versus meditative exercise, and it has been reported that depression responds more readily to the dynamic active exercise in moving energy through the meridian system.

It was not our intent to measure for a significant drop of blood pressure, as this was not in keeping with safety guidelines of the experiment with regard to subjects. The intent was to make an observation of a change in blood pressure, specifically a lowering of readings, after the qi emission treatment. Most definitely, qigong exercise would be an advisable treatment for those who suffer from high blood pressure. It should be noted that most practitioners will generally spend an hour with an individual seeking treatment, and our time limitation of 10 minutes precluded a full assessment and treatment of the subject according to normal TCM guidelines and practice procedure.

Based on the results of the research study, I can readily say that qigong can be a very effective application in the treatment of depression, and that if used consistently over a long period of time, the potential for bringing the body back into balance and harmony is greater. No psychotherapy or counseling was provided to subjects during this experiment in order to measure specifically for the effects of the qigong exercise. It would be my expectation that qigong exercise as a complementary and alternative treatment along with psychotherapy would increase the effectiveness of the body to move energy and to enhance the recovery process by opening the channels of neurochemistry.

The belief that the exercise was helping was a major predictor in how well the subjects did. This poses the rhetorical question of the chicken and the egg; if I believe it is helpful, I will continue to do the exercise; if I don't, I will not do the exercise. By doing the exercise, one can open energy centers and be motivated to provide the adequate neurochemistry to move from the debilitating darkness of depression, building upon the daily feeling of wellness. A belief in the unlimited resource and that it is accessible is the basic premise of the technique.

The placebo factor should be considered, in that the subjects participating in a clinical study may be affected in several ways. First, the study itself creates an aura of self importance and the Hawthorne effect may be responsible for some of the improvement. Second, the dramatic setting of the treatment center brought a certain weight to the expectations of the results. Third, so too did the participation of the expert practitioner from the Mayo Clinic who designed the technique. Fourth, access to a mysterious Chinese treatment used by millions in the East also heightened expectations.

Follow-up study

No formal follow-up study was conducted; however, I did meet and talk with numerous participants at a later date. One participant, a young man who had been suffering from a serious and life-threatening illness, presented for treatment with me at a following date some two years later. His medical crisis was past; however, he was still being monitored and was considered to be in treatment by his physician. He came to see me not specifically for depression, but more importantly for our purposes here, he had discontinued doing the qigong exercise. He took the SCL-90 test again at this later date, to determine what, if anything, was going on with the symptoms, as I find this a useful protocol for assessment.

He has graciously consented to the publication of his test scores, which indicate the measures on all of the various SCL-90 scales at the initial three test administrations while a subject in the study, as well as the follow-up date two years later, when he was no longer doing qigong. See Figure 7.9

The test dates are located in the upper right-hand corner, and are indicated on the graphs by the point marks. The scores are indicated as T-scores. As you can readily observe, the scores declined rapidly over the initial treatment period of two months from a high clinical profile, to a less distressed level. Over the two-year period following the experiment, and when he was not doing the qigong exercise, the scores increased; however, they did not approach the initial distressed level. Granted, he was no longer in medical danger, but he was still in the treatment process with the possibility of relapse. He was right to seek advice once again, and we both agreed that he should resume the qigong exercise immediately. I am pleased to report that he is doing very well at time of writing.

Suggestions for further research

Further research on this subject could be benefited by the use of greater technical measures by way of EEG, PET scan and tools which measure magnetic resonance. I had thought about doing a

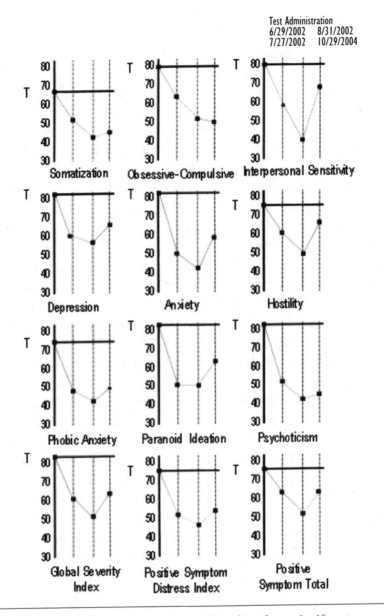

Figure 7.9 SCL-90 scores of test subject show that a significant improvement occurred during the study period from 6/29/2002 until 8/31/2002 as a result of the qigong exercise; after the study, the exercise was discontinued and, after a two-year period, the SCL-90 scores had increased, but not to the initial high levels at the 6/29/2002 measure

Kirlian photograph of the individuals before and after the experiment just to satisfy curiosity, but costs were a consideration. A more homogeneous group could be useful in obtaining measures, and utilizing a true control group would better control for placebo factors. An experiment which incorporates a standardized level of pathology of depression (BDI or SCL-90) as well as those not suffering from depression could be utilized with groups that receive real qi emission as well as imitation qi emission.

The three individuals who had a bipolar diagnosis did improve in this experiment and it is suggested that further inquiry be made into the ability of qigong to balance the flow of neurotransmitters in creating greater balance within this DSM category. Research should be conducted with anger management and substance-addicted groups, as the increase of alpha in the frontal lobe area and decrease of blood flow in the limbic system suggest that qigong would be an appropriate treatment modality. A study conducted with those who suffer from attention deficit disorder would also be appropriate.

A reduction of all symptom indices of the SCL-90 was observed including anxiety, obsessive compulsive, hostility, phobia, paranoia and psychoticism and it would be beneficial to examine the usefulness of qigong in each of these pathologies. A study utilizing qigong as an adjunct to psychotherapy, specifically cognitive behavioral techniques, is suggested to provide a comprehensive mind-body treatment format.

· *Appendix 1* ·

ACTIVE EXERCISES

Spring Forest Qigong Active Exercises are from the manual by Chunyi Lin (2000).

DVDs are available at www.SpringForestQigong.com.

Main benefits of exercises

There are five main benefits of these exercises:

- to strengthen your physical energy

- to help you open all energy channels in the body

- to help you bring your yin and yang energy back into balance

- to help you get rid of energy blockages

- to help you develop your spiritual energy so that you heal yourself physically, mentally and spiritually at the same time.

Do the Active Exercises at least once daily.

When doing the Active Exercises without the DVD for guidance, you can do any combination of the individual exercises for any amount of time. There are no maximum time limits. You may want to take a break during sessions lasting more than two hours. You can practice this exercise by sitting or lying down.

Eight Active Exercises

The Active Exercises open all your energy channels by using your mind and moving your hands, feet and body.

This series consists of the following exercises, which are described in detail throughout Chunyi Lin's course manual:

1. Beginning of the Universe

2. Forming of Yin and Yang

3. Moving of Yin and Yang

4. Breathing of the Universe

5. Joining of Yin and Yang

6. Harmony of Universal Energy

7. Seven Steps of New Life

8. Ending: Harvesting Qi.

Beginning of the Universe

To bring your focus back into your body and wake up the internal energy.

Time on DVD: 2–3 minutes.

Time to do on your own: 2–3 minutes.

The energy channels in the feet and the hands wake up. You may notice tingling sensations in your fingers and feet.

There are many energy channels in the body, but the most important ones are the front channel and the back channel. The front channel runs through the front and middle of the body; the back channel runs along the spine to the head.

All the other channels work around these two channels. A blockage in these two channels will result in a problem in the body.

When you practice this exercise, place your tongue against the roof of your mouth. Your tongue acts as the switch connecting the two channels.

- When doing this exercise standing, stand straight. Toes pointing forward.

- Set your feet a little more than shoulder width apart for good balance. Eyes look forward.

- Wear a smile on your face to relax every part of the body and stimulate the brain to produce endorphins.

- Draw your chin back a little to straighten the entire spine. Energy travels up and down the spine in the governing channel more easily when the spine is straight. Open your fingers. Drop the shoulders. Move the elbows outward a little.

- Slowly take a deep, silent and gentle breath through your nose. As you breathe in, draw the lower part of your stomach in a little. As you breathe out, let your stomach out.

- Imagine using your whole body to breathe. Visualize the universal energy coming into every cell of your body and collecting in the lower dantian. This is the body's primary energy center located deep behind the navel.

- When you exhale, visualize any pain or sickness changing into smoke and shooting out from every cell of your body to the end of the universe.

- Gently close your eyes and lips. And say in your mind:

  I am in the universe. The universe is in my body. The universe and I combine together.

- Feel the emptiness, the quietness, and the stillness of the universe.

Forming of Yin and Yang

Hold this posture to rebalance the energy.
Time on DVD: 3 minutes.
Time to do on your own: 3–5 minutes.

The upper part of the torso above the navel belongs to yang. The lower part of the torso under the navel belongs to yin. One of the

reasons people get sick is because the yin and yang energies scatter and are not in good balance.

You will feel tingly sensations in your hands and warmth in the chest and lower stomach, which are areas faced by your palms. You may also feel a current running in the middle of the torso or along the spine, which are the energy channels opening.

- Slowly raise your right hand, the yang male energy, to the upper chest and your left hand, the yin female energy, to the lower stomach. Your palms face your body, without touching, to create a sensation of emptiness.

- Visualize a transparent energy column in the middle of your torso shining with beautiful colors. It runs from the head to the bottom of the torso. Its size depends on your visualization.

- Continue to feel the emptiness of the universe as you remain in this position.

- When you hold your hands in this posture, drop your elbows. Stand still so that energy flows uninterrupted.

Moving of Yin and Yang

To heal internal organs.
Time on DVD: 13 minutes.
Time to do on your own: 10–60 minutes.

Through the guidance of our mind and the movement of our hands, the heart energy and the kidney energy join. Blockages open.

- Your right hand moves out and down to the bottom of your torso while your left hand moves in and up to your face. Your hands continue moving in this circular pattern.

- Visualize a transparent energy column of beautiful colors running from the top of the head to the bottom of the torso. While moving your hands, visualize the energy moving up and down the transparent column. Visualize the channels in the torso opening completely.

- Use your elbows to guide the movements and use your hands to feel the energy.

- Your hands move at the rate of three to five circles each minute.

- Keep your fingers open to receive energy. Your energy channels close when your fingers close.

Tip: Do not move your spine from side to side, even when you feel tired, because that movement stops your energy from going to the emptiness level.

Moving of Yin and Yang is the basic movement of the Active Exercise in Level I.

Breathing of the Universe

To heal the lungs and skin, and balance energy inside and outside of the body.

Time on DVD: 6 minutes.

Time to do on your own: 6–30 minutes.

By moving your hands out and in and combining the breathing technique, you open blockages in the whole body, especially the lungs.

As you finish the Moving of Yin and Yang, both hands slowly stop at the lower dantian position. For men, put your left hand in and right hand out; for women, it's right hand in and left hand out.

- There is a space between the body and the hands and between both hands. In this way you can keep the feeling of emptiness.

- Focus on your lower dantian. Take three deep breaths.

- Then as you inhale, move your hands open to the sides; exhale as you close your hands.

- Use your whole body to breathe.

When you open your hands, try to feel the energy as it expands in the space between your hands. When you close your hands, try to feel the energy being compressed in the space between your hands. Your hands do not touch each other.

- Use your hands and body to feel the energy while you use the elbows to guide the action.

- While you inhale, visualize the pure universal energy flowing into your body from every part of the body and gathering in the lower dantian.

- While you exhale, imagine any sickness or pain turning into air or smoke and shooting out from every part of the body to the end of the universe.

- Do not move your neck from side to side. Stay still and relaxed. Wear a smile. Always keep your tongue against the roof of your mouth.

Joining of Yin and Yang

To balance your body's energy.
Time on DVD: 6 minutes.
Time to do on your own: 6–30 minutes.

You build energy in the lower dantian.

As you finish the Breathing of the Universe, imagine your hands coming together around a ball of energy about the size of a soccer ball. Keep your fingers open so the energy can flow. Your palms face each other.

- Start rolling the ball by moving your hands continuously from top to bottom and from bottom to top.

- Imagine your body's energy is in the ball and is being totally renewed.

Harmony of Universal Energy

To open blockages and heal the body and to balance the energy in the left brain and right brain. It will especially help you advance your spiritual energy to a higher level.

Time on DVD: 15 minutes.

Time to do on your own: 15–30 minutes or longer.

By moving hands and body, you open blockages in the lungs, breasts, liver, spine, shoulders, lower back and hips. When you do this movement with your eyes closed, you may see more colors. People who practice Spring Forest Qigong say that this portion of exercise is very useful for waking the body after a restful night's sleep.

1. Receive energy from the universe with your hands.

2. As you inhale, raise the energy ball up in front of you up and over your head. Open your hands and arms wide above your head, palms up, head slightly up.

3. Hold your breath as you bring your hands together. Bring the energy down with your hands to cover your head without touching your head. Hold for three seconds.

4. Exhale and bring your hands down passing the face. As you reach the chin, bring your hands together, palms in, and continue moving your hands down until you come to your lower stomach.

5. Inhale; open your hands wide to the sides as you did in "Breathing of the Universe." Use your elbows to guide the movement and your hands to feel the energy.

6. Exhale as you bring your hands in, collecting more energy.

7. Keep closing your hands until they pass each other and reach to each other's elbow area with your right hand on top first and left hand at the bottom. Your palms face down; hands do not touch the elbows.

8. Inhale; lower your head down and lean forward to the right until your head is over the right elbow without touching the elbow. Your head turns slightly to the left. Remain in this position as you exhale.

9. Inhale, drawing the right hand up and to the right until your arm is straight. The fingers of the right hand continue pointing to the left with the palm facing down. At the same time, our left hand moves out pressing down to the left.

10. Fingers point to the right with the palm down. (This opens all of the six channels in your hands. If you turn your fingers outward, only three channels open.) Lean forward to the right as you raise your left heel up, pointing the toes. (Moving the heels up and down can help open the six channels in the feet.)

11. Exhale as you open the right hand, turn it facing down and smoothly move it down in a circle, as the left hand moves in until you are holding the energy ball between your hands once again. Repeat the circle.

Seven Steps of New Life

To improve the balance and heal the body, especially for arthritis, cold hands and cold feet.

Time on DVD: 10 minutes.

Time to do on your own: 10–30 minutes.

This is the "plunger" technique. Like a bellows, you draw energy into the body, collect it in your lower dantian, and pump it throughout the entire body. It opens and clears all the body's energy channels.

Starting with your left leg, imagine using your whole body as a bellows for moving energy to seven levels.

1. Navel

2. Heart

3. Shoulders

4. Throat

5. Nose

6. Forehead

7. Top of the head.

(Warning: Pregnant women should skip this exercise. The movement of the energy might disturb the peace of the baby.)

- Inhale and visualize universal energy flowing into your body through every cell and collecting in the first level behind the navel.

- Exhale, pushing the energy down to the toes.

- Inhale again, drawing the energy from the toes up to the second level, the heart level.

- Exhale, pushing the energy down to the toes.

- Repeat this process multiple times through all of the levels.

Use your hands to guide the energy. On each inhale, move your hands up to the upper chest with your palms facing up. On each exhale,

move your hands down to your lower torso with your palms facing down.

On each inhale, lift your leg with the toes pointing to the ground. On each exhale, step forward to press your heel to the ground. Always start with your left leg and alternate through the exercise.

You may do as many rounds of the seven levels as you wish. When finished, inhale one more time. Visualize energy flowing into your body and collecting in your lower dantian. Exhale without focusing your mind on anything.

Ending: Harvesting Qi

To adjust energy in the body and to help the body heal and gain back its energy balance faster.

Time on DVD: 10 minutes.

Time to do on your own: 10 minutes.

All of the movements of the Active Exercises can be practiced separately. You might choose one or two movements each day, or you can do them all. Always finish with the Ending Exercise. This will bring you out of your meditation and help put the qi into the right places of your body. When you choose to do Active Exercises and a Sitting Meditation, do the Active Exercises first to make it easier to go into the emptiness. Follow the Sitting Meditation with the Ending Exercise.

1. Rub your hands together, palm to palm.

2. Massage your face. With your palms toward your face, use your middle fingers to push up along the bridge of the nose until your fingers reach the forehead. Cover your face with your hands, and part your hands as they draw down the face to the chin.

3. Comb your head with your fingers from the front to the back of the head. The tips of your fingers must touch your scalp.

4. Form your hands into a cup. Pat your head with your cupped hands from front to back.

5. Massage your ears from top to bottom. Every part of the ear must be massaged.

6. Cup your hands again and pat the inside and outside of each arm.

7. Pat your chest and stomach from top to bottom.

8. Pat your underarm area on the left side and then the right side.

9. Massage your stomach by interlacing your fingers and massage right to left in a clockwise direction.

10. Bend over at the waist. Cup your hands again and pat the kidney area (i.e. at the back, directly above the waistline on both left and right sides). Then, use the back of your hands to massage this area several times. Turn your hands over and massage the kidneys a few more times.

11. Support your kidneys by covering them with your hands and slowly straighten the body by lifting the back and shoulders. Lift the head last.

12. Use your chin to draw a horizontal circle from left to right six times. Repeat in the other direction.

13. Dolphin the neck by moving the head slightly forward and up, then down and back. This is the same as drawing a vertical circle. Do this six times.

14. Support the kidney area with your hands and dolphin the whole spine; move the upper part of the body forward first, bend the knees and move them forward, and extend the stomach, the chest and the head. Do this six times.

15. Straighten the body. Lift your hands up in front of your chest with your palms down and your elbows slightly higher than the shoulders. Look forward. Lead with the elbows and swing your arms from left to right, keeping your head and hips facing forward. Do this six times.

16. Lower the elbows to the stomach level and repeat the swing motion six times. (Be gentle if you have severe lower back problems.)

17. Put your hands down. Lift your body up by stretching the heels up (that is, standing on your toes) and dropping the heels down six times. (Pregnant women should skip this exercise.)

· *Appendix 2* ·

SUPPLEMENTARY EXERCISES

In the Ending Exercise we have movements that involve the spine and massaging and patting the body.

Eight Ending Exercises

1. Massage the hands

2. Massage the face and ears

3. Massage the kidneys

4. Cupping exercise

5. Spine exercise

6. Heel exercise

7. Walking and running exercise

8. Sleeping exercise.

Let's explore why we do these exercises.

Massage the hands

There are six main channels starting from the fingers. For instance, two heart channels start from the middle and the little fingers, and the lung and large intestine channels start from the thumb. When you massage the hands and fingers, you wake up the qi in those channels and it will go into the internal organs.

Massage the face and ears

The face and ears have all the points linking to all energy channels and all parts of the body. When you massage your face and ears, you massage your whole body. If you feel pain when you massage your ears, you have a blockage in the relative part or organ in the body. Keep massaging that point on your ear until the pain is totally gone – the blockage in the body will disappear.

Massage the kidneys

The are to be massaged is the left and right sides directly above the waist, at the back of the body. Kidney energy is the most important energy to our life. If we use up the kidney energy faster, our lives will end sooner. A man's kidney energy goes down after age 40, and a woman's after age 35. Our legs are the first parts of the body to indicate we are aging. When we feel our legs are not as strong as before, our kidney energy is getting low. In Dao meditation, Chinese medicine, and longevity exercises, the kidney energy is always number one in our attention.

Cupping exercise

The areas to be cupped have almost all of the energy channels. Cupping wakes up and moves the energy in those channels and clears away blockages. If you catch a cold, cup your arms to help stop coughing, because the lung, heart, and large intestine channels run through the arms.

Spine exercise

Most human ailments relate to blockages in the spine: mental problems and other sickness in the head relate to the neck; sicknesses in the major organs relate to the back spine; and reproductive organ problems relate to the lower back and the tailbone.

I recommend that women over 35 spend several minutes patting the tailbone area at the base of the spine every day to prevent blockages in the female organs.

Heel exercise

When you move the heels up and down, you open the energy channels in your feet including the liver and kidney channels. This exercise is very good for constipation as well as chilly feet and hands in the cold seasons.

Walking and running exercise

When you walk or run, put your tongue against the roof of the mouth. Swing your hands naturally from side to side with your fingers open and form a yin-yang circle.

As you inhale, imagine the pure universal energy running into the body through every cell and gathering deep in behind the navel. As you exhale, imagine any sickness and all energy blockages change into smoky air and shoot out from every cell to the end of the universe. These exercises can be done any time.

Sleeping exercise

Put your tongue against the roof of the mouth. Inhale and exhale the same as the walking and running exercises. You can sleep on your back or on either side. Do not sleep on your stomach, because your neck will twist and blockages can gradually develop.

Before getting out of bed first thing in the morning, take a deep breath three times, rub your hands, and massage your face. This exercise is especially useful for those who have sleeping problems.

SITTING MEDITATIONS

To open energy channels by developing mental concentration and controlling breathing, practice the two Sitting Meditations.

Two Sitting Meditations

1. Small Universe

2. Self Concentration.

Sit with your spine straight and feet flat on the floor. Place your hands over your knees with your palms up. Keep your fingers extended; otherwise you will fall asleep. If you have high blood pressure, place your hands in your lap with your palms down.

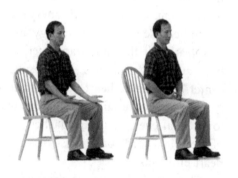

By using mental concentration, controlled breathing and sound, you open the front and back channels.

Small Universe

To clear energy blockages along the front and back channels.
    Time on CD: 30 minutes.
    Time to do on your own: 30–60 minutes.

We have many energy channels and energy centers in our bodies. When energy starts at one point, visits all the channels and centers in the body and comes back to the starting point, we have what is literally translated from Chinese ancient wisdom as a "big universe."

The most important channels are the back and front channels in the torso. When energy starts at one point on those channels, visits all the parts of the system, and comes back to the starting point, we have what is called a "small universe." Many small universes make up a big universe.

The back channel starts at the lower dantian area, which is deep in behind the navel. It goes down to the bottom of the torso, travels up along the spine to the top of the head, and comes down from the middle of the forehead, stopping at the roof of the mouth.

The front channel also starts from the lower dantian area, goes down to the bottom of the torso, travels up the body, passing through the heart and throat, stopping under the tongue.

Those two channels control and influence the other channels in the body. They automatically connect together four hours a day: at noon from 11:00 a.m. to 1:00 p.m. and at midnight from 11:00 p.m. to 1:00 a.m. Qigong practitioners like to meditate at midnight and at noon, because it takes less energy and generates greater benefits.

Nearly all the important energy centers are arranged along the back and front channels. As a result, a blockage in the heart energy center could cause heart, lung, breast, chest or intelligence problems. A blockage in the tailbone could cause reproductive organ problems, low sexual energy, and headaches. A blockage in the cervical bone 7 of the spinal cord could cause headaches, fever, diabetes and lung and heart problems.

The Small Universe is the easiest meditation technique to open these two channels:

- Concentrate your mind in the lower dantian, which is deep in behind the navel.

- Visualize your own energy and all of your generational energy (the energy automatically passed down from generation to generation) joining together, shining very brightly in your lower dantian.

- Listen to the master's voice on the CD. You will hear two sounds: [...OHM...] and [...MUA...].

- These sounds are extremely powerful, because their vibration can reach every corner of the body to clear blockages. Each time you hear the sound, inhale; in between the sounds, exhale.

On each inhale, visualize the master's energy and the universal energy joining together and radiating into an area of your body.

On each exhale, move the energy to the next area of your body. The specific areas of your body are shown here in the photograph.

- Then start all over again from the lower dantian.

- You can continue to move the energy through the Small Universe for as many rounds as you want. But at the end, stop at the lower dantian.

- Visualize the energy as a ball moving clockwise inside the lower dantian. The energy ball gets smaller and smaller, finally changing into an energy pill that hides deep in behind the navel.

- When finished, take a deep breath three times. Rub your hands. Massage your face.

- Comb your hair. Cup your head. Massage your ears.

- Move your head from left to right in a circular way six times and then do it the other way six times.

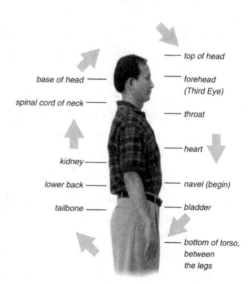

base of head —

spinal cord of neck —

— top of head

— forehead (Third Eye)

— throat

— heart

kidney —

lower back —

tailbone —

— navel (begin)

— bladder

— bottom of torso, between the legs

Self Concentration

To heal the body and develop personal self awareness.
Time on CD: 30 minutes.
Time to do on your own: 30–60 minutes.

By using mental concentration and controlled breathing, you move to a deeper level of meditation.

- Listen to the tape.

- Wear a smile on your face.

- Take three deep breaths, inhaling through your nose and exhaling through your mouth to clear away toxins in the stomach.

- Say in your mind the password:

  I am in the universe. The universe is in my body. The universe and I combine together.

- Say in your mind:

  All my channels open, open, open, completely open. I have no energy blockages in my body. All my pains are gone. I am completely healed.

- Feel your whole spine, starting from the tailbone, growing longer, straighter, longer, straighter, even straighter, completely straight.

- Feel all the channels within your body open: the head channels, the neck channels, the stomach channels, the lower back channels, the tailbone channels, the channels at the bottom of the torso, the thigh channels, the leg channels, and the feet channels.

- Feel all the blockages in the lungs, liver and pancreas change into smoke and disappear. All of the stones within the body explode and turn into smoke and disappear. All of the tumors within the body turn into smoke and completely disappear. Visualize the inside of your body as clean and healthy.

- Imagine that you are in the season of spring as a happy little girl or boy, running on the green grass. The air is fresh, sun is warm, trees are green, water is blue, and the flowers are beautiful. Birds are singing sweetly. Children are playing. You have no worry, sadness, sorrow, depression or stress. You feel safe, peaceful and relaxed. All your burdens are gone. Love, kindness and forgiveness are all coming back to you. You feel happy and healthy, totally lost in the harmony of the universe.

- When finished, take a deep breath three times. Rub your hands. Massage your face. Cup your head. Massage your ears.

In addition, I recommend that you do the Active Exercises, any component of the Active Exercises, or one of the Sitting Meditations at least twice a week for one hour. May I strongly recommend that you do the exercises or meditations at least once a day. You will receive more benefit if you can do it three times each day, especially if you have severe blockages in your body.

The best time for exercise and meditation is whenever you can fit them into your schedule. Beyond that we find the best times for doing the Active Exercises are in the morning and early in the evening. The best times for the Sitting Meditations are in the morning, at noon and in the late evening around midnight, because the energy during those times is more balanced.

Typical reactions

Typical reactions and sensations while practicing Spring Forest Qigong may include the following:

- itching on your body

- tingling sensations

- seeing colors

- smelling incense or lotus flower – this is your master's energy or spiritual energy coming to help you

- breeze

- heat running inside your body

- electricity flowing through your body

- hearing unknown sounds

- automatic movement of the body

- crying or tearing.

Another reaction is to feel sadness. This sadness is not for something specific, but is for the whole universe. This means your soul energy has awakened; it is a very powerful healing energy.

Some people find their pains or symptoms worsening. This can happen to those who have arthritis or structural damage after accidents. It indicates energy is trying to heal the body and bringing the body to its normal condition. The pain usually does not stay long. Only 10 percent of people who have arthritis or structural problems experience more pain. When this happens, please call your doctor for advice before continuing the exercise.

Helpful tips

- Get the advice of a medical doctor before beginning this or any other exercise program.

- Follow the instructions contained in the Spring Forest Qigong Personal Learning Manual.

- Avoid mixing Spring Forest Qigong movements with other energy techniques.

- When you do qigong exercises, especially the Active Exercises, do not move your hands and legs too fast. The slower, the better.

- Do not have anything cold to drink 30 minutes before you do the exercise. The cold energy will interfere with the flowing of the qi.

- Do not eat 30 minutes before or after the exercise. The digestion process will absorb energy that otherwise would be used for healing.

- Do not do the exercise when you are too excited or too emotional, because it is difficult to focus, quiet the mind, and go into the emptiness.

- Do not use the bathroom within 30 minutes after the exercise because you will lose qi.

- Do not use alcohol before or after the exercise because alcohol depletes qi and affects the mind.

- Do not do the exercise outside in the rain, wind or snow.

- Do not exercise when there is a thunderstorm, because the storm makes it difficult to go into the emptiness.

- Neither wash your hands and face with cold water nor take a bath immediately after the exercise because you will lose qi and you may get ill.

- Wear comfortable clothes that do not constrict the body.

- Be free from distractions such as the telephone.

Help others heal

You can use qi to heal yourself. You can also use qi to help others, because the principles are the same. You will find it easy and simple to send energy out to help others heal.

A long time ago, I asked different qigong masters how long it would take to learn to heal others. Some said 10 years, some said 15 years, some even said 50 years.

I have learned it takes only two minutes! Follow my instruction and try it today.

- First, hold your fingers in a position called sword fingers. The tips of the little and ring fingers touch the first part of the thumb. The middle and index fingers rest together and point straight out.

- Point the sword fingers toward an area where your friend feels pain or discomfort (you will learn how to detect blockages in Level Two). Move the sword fingers around to break up the energy blockages. (Do not point sword fingers to the heart, because the frequency of the energy does not agree with the heart's energy.)

- Open your fingers. Visualize energy shooting out from your fingers – you can use both hands or one. Energy goes into the part of the body where it has blockages whether pain, a stone, or a tumor.

- Visualize the energy changing blockages into air or smoke. Take hold of the air or smoke. Move it out of the body and throw it to the earth. This energy blockage is extra energy on the body that you return to the universe. Keep pulling the air out until you feel the blockage is clear. (Do not pull energy from the top of the head or the front of the torso in front of the heart. This is discussed in considerable detail in Level Two.)

- While you are pulling out the blockage, repeat in your mind, "Blockages open. Pains are gone. You are completely healed." Say that loudly with great confidence in your mind.

- Use your palm(s) to give healing energy back to the area where you removed the blockage by moving your hand in and out nine times – wear a smile on your face. Move your hand(s) gently, because the energy will be more comforting.

In Spring Forest healing, the more energy you send out to heal others, the more you will receive.
The keys are:

- Always call upon your master's energy to tap a tremendous resource. When your master's energy joins your energy, you will have much more energy to use.

- While you are doing the healing, visualize universal energy coming into your body through every cell and gathering in your lower dantian. In this way, you collect more energy during the healing than you send.

- At the end, ask your friend to take three deep breaths, rub his hands, and massage his face. These movements help him come out of the meditation without feeling spacey.

- Say: "You feel great now!" or "You feel better now!" Never ask: "Do you still feel the pain?" This will cause your friend to search for the pain and bring it back.

- You can also use sword fingers to heal yourself.

- To make your healing more effective, have faith. Trust the universal energy. Trust the spiritual energy.

Feel confident. Focus on how much you love people; not on success or failure. Embrace your eagerness to help friends. Focus on the honorable opportunity you have as you help yourself grow. Visualize the sickness, pain and discomfort as smoke. Or be creative and come up with another visualization to focus the power of your mind.

The stronger your focus and visualization, the more successful your healing.

GLOSSARY

Acupressure. An ancient healing art in which gentle, firm pressure from the fingers, feet or elbows is applied to the surface of the skin at the acupuncture points along the meridian system.

Acupuncture. An ancient Chinese method of treating disease or relieving pain by inserting one or more metal needles into the body at certain critical meridian points in the meridian system. A high electrical conductivity exists at these points and, when stimulated, the electrical signal sent through the meridians intensifies the healing process and decreases pain. Acupuncture is now accepted as a viable treatment in Western medicine.

Acupuncture points. *See* **meridian points**.

Alpha, beta and theta waves. Waves created by the pulsation and vibration of the brain. Alpha (8–13 Hz cycles per second) appears when in wakefulness there is a relaxed and effortless alertness. Light meditation and day dreaming, creative visualization and auto-suggestion occur in the alpha range. Beta (13–40 Hz cycles per second) is associated with our waking activity and this is the predominant pattern. Theta (4–7 Hz cycles per second) waves are associated with creativity, dreams and extra-sensory perception. A fourth wave, Delta (½–4 Hz cycles per second), is associated with deep sleep.

ATP (Adenosine 5' triphosphate). The cell's molecular energy source. The hydrolysis of ATP molecules to produce adenosine diphosphase (ADP) releases energy that fuels most of the neuron's biochemical reactions. ADP is converted back to ATP in the mitochondria of the neuron. The human body turns over its own weight in ATP each day.

Ayurvedic medicine. Sanskrit for "life science," a system of traditional medicine native to India and practiced as a form of alternative medicine. Methods include the use of herbs, massage, meditation and yoga application. Ayurveda stresses a balance of a healthy metabolic system, good digestion and proper excretion which leads to vitality.

Biodynamic massage. Deep pressure is used to relieve muscles that are tensed by repeated or chronic conflicts and affecting energy flow. Utilizing an in-depth awareness of the body as embodiment of a psychological and energetic system, a skilled practitioner senses energetic changes in the area and works the massage pressure until a change is felt. A useful treatment for stress, psychosomatic symptoms, or as an adjunct to psychotherapy.

Biodynamic psychotherapy. Developed in the 1950s by Gerda Boyesen, a Norwegian psychologist, and based on a deep appreciation of the inseparable interaction of mind, body and spirit. The core objective is to help the person to reconnect with their primary potential, without the obstacle of negative effects of the repressed memory. It incorporates verbal psychotherapy, emotional expression work and psychotherapeutic body work by "releasing" the memories and feelings which are stored in the body.

Bioenergetics. An active area of biological research concerned with energy flow through living systems. It includes the study of different cellular processes such as cellular respiration and many other metabolic processes that can lead to production and utilization of energy in forms such as ATP molecules.

Biofeedback. A technique which involves measuring an individual's quantifiable bodily functions (such as blood pressure, heart rate, skin temperature, sweat gland activity, and muscle tension) and relaying this information back to the individual in real time. The raised awareness of physiological processes enables the individual to gain conscious control over activities previously considered unconscious, automatic responses of the autonomous nervous system.

Breathing exercises. The increase of oxygen has an immediate and long-term effect on the physiology. Exercises range from simply focusing on the breath, to deeper and more complex techniques such as holotropic integration, and qigong or Tantric breathing which serve to move energy through the body.

Chakra. Sanskrit for "wheel" or "disc," a wheel-like vortex which is a center of activity that receives, assimilates and expresses life force energy. There are six main chakras on the body, stacked in a column from the base of the spine to the middle of the forehead, with a seventh situated above the head. The chakras correlate with basic states of consciousness and regulate distinct aspects of personality. The lower chakras (below the waist) are concerned with the physical animal functions of the body – survival, sex and power – and the upper chakras with higher forms of consciousness, such as intelligent speech, wisdom and joy. The heart chakra, which sits between them, is said to be the transforming compassionate vehicle in the development of consciousness.

Chi Nei Tsang. A qigong technique developed by Daoist and Buddhist monks for internal organ energy transformation, involving gentle manipulation of the intestinal tract to cultivate internal energy. Gilles Marin brought the technique to the United States (Marin 1999; Post and Cavaliere 2003).

Chiron holistic psychotherapy. The Chiron Centre is a private institute in West London. The therapy incorporates body psychotherapy, along with a holistic, integrative, relational and humanistic approach.

Cognitive dissonance. The feelings of discomfort and tension which come from holding two conflicting thoughts in the mind at the same time, usually involving the individual's attitudes and beliefs and the awareness of his or her behavior. Conflicting ideas about the self increase anxiety and the result-ant dissonance can lead to bias and denial, such as "Smoking helps to curb my appetite." According to social psychology, there is a motivational drive to reduce the difference or dissonance between new information and exist-ing attitudes and beliefs. So when logical new information does not fit into the individual's schema or belief pattern, that person may justify his or her existing behavior by changing the conflicting cognition or interpreting it differently, adding new cognitions, or by changing their existing behavior.

Daoism. Also spelled Taoism. An Eastern philosophy of thought with a core of beliefs based upon the revelations of Lao Tzu. Daoism emphasizes themes for guiding behavior such as naturalness, vitality, peace, *wu wei* (non-action), emptiness, refinement, detachment, flexibility and spontaneity. *See also* **The Way**.

Dialectical behavior therapy (DBT). A psychological treatment developed by Marsha M. Linehan, a psychology researcher at the University of Washington, to treat individuals suffering from borderline personality disorder (BPD), and found to be the first effective deterrent to suicidal ideation and attempt. Treatment includes behaviorist theory, cognitive therapy and the component of mindfulness taken from Buddhist meditative practice. It is effective for treating BPD as it trains the individual to increase his or her capacity for distress tolerance, thereby reducing self-injurious behavior.

Dolphin the neck. To extend the head and neck slightly up and forward (as a dolphin jumps out of the water) and then to move it back, slowly and gracefully.

Electroacupuncture (EA). The same meridian points are stimulated during treatment as in traditional acupuncture, but the needles are attached to a device that generates continuous electrical pulses. EA is particularly useful for treating pain, and has been used on musculoskeletal trauma, muscle dys-function, and over-use injuries such as tendinitis, spasms and sprains.

Elixir field. The pattern of movement of the qi (life force) as it moves down the front and up the back of the torso, providing energy to the organs along the way. It is perceivable to the qi master as a vapor.

Energy field. A complex network of interwoven energy fields that operate within and around the body. Also known as the aura, the energy field represents the spirit, a luminous force which surrounds and penetrates the body emitting its own characteristic radiation and vibration. The meridian system and chakras are affected by this field as the frequency and intensity of the signals transmitted and received by the human body resonate with certain thoughts and emotions. For example, coherence in the wave patterns of an electrocardiogram creates harmony in the individual's nervous, hormonal and immune systems.

Energy medicine. The term has been in general use since the founding of the International Society for the Study of Subtle Energies and Energy Medicine (ISSSEEM) in the 1980s. Energy therapies fall into two categories. (1) Putative energy medicine utilizes forms of "energy" unknown to current science; therapies include acupuncture, qigong and related concepts involving the notion of qi, such as Reiki, polarity therapy, homeopathy, acupuncture and Therapeutic Touch. (2) Veritable energy medicine relies on known forms of energy, such as electromagnetism.

External qi. *See* **wai qi**.

Guided imagery. A technique of actively directing thoughts and suggestions while in a relaxed focused state. A qualified, trained instructor uses CDs or scripts to assist in the process. The relaxed state can aid in healing, learning and performance. It can lower blood pressure, reduce stress, improve attitude and help to manifest a state of well-being. It is a safe technique which can be very useful and pleasurable.

Hawthorne effect. A form of reactivity detected by Henry A. Landsberger in 1955 when analyzing experiments conducted at the Hawthorne Works in Chicago. A short-term improvement in performance triggered when individuals know they are being observed or paid special attention as part of a study group or team.

Heart constrictor. TCM term for the pericardium, the heart's protective sack. Believed to protect against shock and hurt, so when it is unwell, hurt and anxiety can occur more easily.

Holographic Memory Resolution. An energy psychology technique developed by Brent Baum while working with thousands of trauma subjects from the Oklahoma Bombing, 9/11, torture victims and veterans from the Iraq War. The technique is based on the notion that negatively charged experiences can become "frozen" as a hologram within the mind and the physical body and this creates problems such as post-traumatic stress, illness or other neurosis. Practicing it involves sensing the blockage with the hands, and facilitating the memory in a light meditative trance which allows the conscious mind to relax and opening a safe window into the subconscious. Guided visualization using color creates a self-healing process to reframe the experience and lock in positive changes into the subconscious, the body and the energy field. The process can provide a rapid resolution of the memory and its impact on the physical body.

Holotropic integration. From the Greek root meaning "moving toward wholeness." A psychotherapeutic form of breath work with goals of wholeness, healing and wisdom developed by Stanislav Grof, M.D., Ph.D., and Christina Grof. It achieves non-ordinary states of consciousness, which amplify a person's psychic process and facilitate the psyche's natural capacity for healing. Certified facilitators provide information and a format for the breathing that includes evocative music, a reciprocating partnership in sitting and breathing sessions, art, focused energy release work and group sharing for integration.

Hypnosis. A mental state usually induced by a relaxation procedure known as hypnotic induction. It is often misconceived as a form of sleep or being unaware and unconscious; however, it is actually a wakened state of focused attention and heightened suggestibility with diminished peripheral awareness.

Inferiority complex. A psychological sense of inferiority that is either wholly or partly unconscious. The concept was initiated by Alfred Adler (1870–1937) who held that neurotic symptoms were related to feelings of inferiority initiated in childhood. The child feels small and helpless and desires to grow in order to become as powerful as the adults around him; therefore the inferiority complex provides the impetus to develop the life goal.

Infrared thermovision. The ability to detect and measure thermal energy emitted from an object. It is accomplished through the use of an infrared camera which translates the invisible thermal images that cannot be detected by the human eye.

Kirlian imaging. A process discovered by Semyon Kirlian in 1939 in which an object on a photographic plate is subjected to a high-voltage electric field, and an image resembling a colored halo or coronal discharge is created on the plate. It is purported to be a physical manifestation of the spiritual aura or life force of every living thing. The process has been researched with homeopathic and acupuncture techniques by Dr. Terry Tobin at the Pasadena College of Chiropractic Medicine, who observed a change in the image before and after treatment. Thelma Moss popularized Kirlian photography as a diagnostic tool with her book *The Body Electric* (1979).

Kirlian photograph. The photograph taken using the Kirlian imaging process. *See also* **Kirlian imaging**.

Kundalini. From the Sanskrit word meaning "the coiled serpent." It is a corporeal energy which may be awakened through meditation, breath work and yoga, and rises up a channel in the spine to the head, bringing psychological illumination. It usually is done under the instruction of a guru. The psycho-analyst Carl Jung used Kundalini yoga as a concept for the development of higher consciousness.

Meditation. A technique in which concentrated focus is used to quiet the conscious mind and draw the attention inward. Focusing on the breath is a useful and readily available technique. There are many different types of meditation, including Christian, Zen, Tibetan and Hindu variations.

Meridian points. Acupuncture meridians are the pathways along which vital energy runs throughout the body. They are generally named for the life function associated with them, and regulate the subtle energy system which carries neurotransmitter communication and qi between various parts of the body. The points are electro-magnetic in character and consist of small palpable spots which may be located by hand, using micro-electrical voltage meters, and with muscle testing.

Meridian system. In traditional Chinese medicine, the distribution network for the fundamental substances of qi. The pathways make up a complex body map that supplies vital energy to every part of the body. Philosophically, the meridian system explains how we live, and why we become ill.

Mind-body problem. In philosophy, the mind-body dichotomy is the starting point of Dualism, and was first philosophically conceptualized by Descartes in the quote "I think, therefore I am." The absence of an empirically identifiable meeting point between the non-physical mind and its physical extension points to Descartes' error and the problem. Modern philosophers of mind claim that the mind and body are integrated, and this understanding has influenced modern science and medicine, resulting in treatments such as biofeedback.

Moxibustian therapy. Uses herbs and heat at various acupuncture points to move energy and speed the healing process.

Neck vertebra Cervical 7. The cervical vertebrae are located in the spine and comprise the bony axis of the neck. Although these are the smallest of the vertebrae, their bone tissues are denser than those in other regions of the spinal column. The cervical neck vertebrae are the top 7 vertebrae in the spinal column and are designated C1 through C7, from the top down. Cervical 7 is located at the base of the neck.

Organ inferiority. A theory developed by Adler, who proposes that the experience of childhood illness can lead to a sense of inferiority, resulting in an inability to compete, withdrawal from society or desire for perfection. In Adlerian theory, "organ jargon" is a term to describe the physical manifestation of emotional problems in various organs of the body (i.e. "a pain in the neck" could be the result of a problematic relationship).

Original mind. The mind before socialization or that which is imposed upon us by culture. In Buddhism, it is described as a clear mirror, pure and uncluttered, without shape, form or color. The goal of meditation is to experience original mind. Likened to our original nature, in this state we are pure, devoid of gender, age and class, close to a metaphorical understanding of the term "enlightenment."

Polarity therapy. A holistic alternative health system developed in the 1940s by Randolph Stone. Based on the principle that the top and right side of the body are positively charged, the feet and left side negatively charged, and the stomach neutral, the technique manipulates these polarized forces to balance and restore the natural flow of energy in the body. Practitioners use a combination of techniques including touch (massage and acupuncture), stretching and exercise, diet and counseling.

Postural integration. A technique to balance and optimize structure, shape and function in the entire body. Deep massage, acupressure, gestalt therapy and the theories of Ida Rolf are applied to release blocked body energies, restoring feelings and awareness. Through the correction of soft tissue asymmetries, the person may gain height, stand straighter and move better.

Qigong state. A deep state of relaxation and mental focus, achieved through the careful regulation of breath, bodily movement and posture. The qigong state is characterized by a balanced coordination of the healing and health-sustaining resources in the body, including immune function, oxygen distribution, lymphatic flow, autonomic balance and the ample and free-flowing activity of the body vitality which the Chinese call qi.

Qigongized paper. Paper believed to release the healing ability of the qi.

Reichian body work. A therapy developed by William Reich to release suppressed emotional traumas. The theory postulates that, as part of our development, "body armor" or muscular contractions manifest as a protective defensive device, and that these may represent blockages to full expression of emotion and balanced energy flow. The Reichian therapist seeks to dissolve or dismantle this body armor. Strategies include therapeutic dialogue, dream work, massage, deep breath work, crying, screaming or rolling of the eyes. Also known as orgone therapy and bio-psychotherapy.

Reiki. From the Japanese root meaning "spiritually guided life force energy," Reiki is a technique for stress reduction and relaxation which promotes healing. A typical treatment involves the qualified practitioner placing their hands upon the body at fixed positions and allowing them to remain there for several minutes while in a meditative state. The patient often feels warmth, tingling or even a surge of movement within the body, followed by a state of deep relaxation and a general feeling of well-being.

Relaxation response (RR). A state of deep rest that changes the physical and emotional responses to stress, slowing the breathing and heartbeat, decreasing blood pressure and the metabolism, relaxing muscles and increasing levels of nitric oxide. The relaxation response is elicited by meditative techniques, deep breathing, imagery, progressive muscle relaxation, repetitive prayer, and physical exercises such as qigong and yoga. If practiced regularly, it can have lasting positive physiological and emotional effects.

Repetitive prayer. The repetition of a personal mantra, such as the word "Ohm," a Tibetan chant, or saying the Rosary. It is a conscious meditative effort which becomes effortless in seeking solace beyond oneself, irrespective of religiosity.

Rolfing. A system of physical structural integration founded by Ida Rolf in the 1950s. The theory maintains that bound-up connective tissue or fascia restricts opposing muscles from functioning in concert with one another. The practice aims to separate the restricted fascia through intensive tissue manipulation.

Schema. A cognitive framework which forms a world view. The concept posits that everyday situations do not require effortful thought because they become automatic through the schema or world view. As a result, when new information is perceived that does not fit a schema, the individual can simply ignore or quickly forget the new information. However, when the information cannot be ignored, the existing schemata must be changed. The schema is the basis for cognitive behavioral therapy.

Seven sites of the chakras (the sites of alchemy energy transfer). Seven centers of spiritual energy in the body. The chakras are differentiated by their location, color and appearance. They should be neither underactive, nor overactive, which purportedly can cause specific emotional or physical difficulties. The root chakra, represented by the color red, is located at the base of the torso, between the anus and genitalia. The sacral chakra, represented by the color orange, is located at the sacral bone on the lower back. The navel chakra is located on the spine, slightly higher than the navel, and is represented by the color yellow. The heart chakra is at the level of the heart, at the spine, and is represented by the color green. The throat chakra is at the base of the throat, at the spine, and is represented by a light blue color. The third eye chakra is located between the eyebrows, slightly above at the forehead, and is represented by a deep blue color. When the chakras have been balanced, developed and opened by raising the consciousness in ascending order, the open "third eye" chakra may provoke enhanced intuitiveness. The crown chakra is located just above the head and is represented by the color white or violet. It is commonly known as the wisdom chakra, representing the spirituality of the higher consciousness. See also **chakra**.

Shamanism. A range of traditional beliefs and practices encouraging interaction with the spirit world. Through the use of fasting, drumming, dancing and singing, the shaman plays the role of healer, and may gain knowledge and power by surmounting a serious illness or psychological crisis. There are many variations throughout the world, as diverse indigenous cultures such as Mayans, Eskimos, Africans, Native Americans and Asians practice shamanism.

Shiatsu. A Japanese massage technique using the fingers, palms and especially the thumbs to apply pressure to particular sections (acupressure points) on the surface of the body to correct imbalances and promote health. It may be useful to stimulate the immune system, calm an overactive nervous system, improve circulation and alleviate stress, and has been shown to be effective in contributing to the healing of specific illnesses.

Social interest. The importance of a sense of connection with the social community. According to Adlerian theory, a lack of social concern is the essence of poor mental health. Thus, Adler stressed the importance of social feeling, not just with respect to social behaviors, but in the broader sense of caring for family, community, society, humanity and life.

Spontaneous dynamic qigong (SDQ). Shaking out trauma and releasing emotion through intuitive movements. Humans hold the emotion in their body, so spontaneous movements such as wiggling, shaking or bouncing after sitting for a long time allows energy or qi to move through the body.

Synchronization phenomenon. During healing sessions, the brain waves of the healer and the recipient enter a state of coherence and synchrony, as if they were unified in a single energy field. This unity has been shown to raise the level of hemoglobin in the recipient's blood, reduce the severity of pain, lower anxiety and heal wounds more rapidly.

Tai chi. An internal Chinese martial art which is generally practiced today for health reasons. It is a series of slow, graceful motions characterized by the use of leverage through the joints based on coordination in relaxation, rather than muscular tension. The circulatory system opens through repetition as the body learns how that leverage is generated and increased. In tai chi, each movement flows into the next and the entire body is always in motion. Breathing and meditation are also important elements, much as in qigong.

The Way. Personified by the ancient Chinese philosopher Lao Tzu, The Way is a path emphasizing compassion, moderation and humility and focusing on nature, health and longevity.

Therapeutic Touch (TT). Developed in the 1970s by Dora Kunz, a promoter and one-time president of the Theosophical Society of America, and Dolores Krieger, Ph.D., R.N., nursing educator at New York University. A technique based on the ancient art of "laying on of hands" without religious associations. The healer or therapist acts as a human energy support system until the recipient's own immunological system is robust enough to take over. The American Holistic Nurses Association endorses TT.

Third eye. Also known as the "inner eye" or the "mind's eye." Located at the sixth chakra, the third eye is said to expand up to the middle of the forehead when opened, increasing intuition. It is often associated with visions, clairvoyance and precognition. The third eye is used in many meditation schools such as yoga, qigong, Zen and the martial arts in order to tune into the right vibration of the universe and gain a solid and balanced foundation into more advanced meditation levels. In the Kabbalah, the third eye chakra corresponds to non-emanated knowledge and wisdom.

Transcendental Meditation™. A trademarked meditation technique introduced by Maharish Mahesh Yogi in 1958. Yogi described it as a mental procedure that allows the mind to quiet itself. The technique involves sitting for 20 minutes twice a day with one's eyes closed while focusing on a selected mantra. This allows the mind to be directed from its natural active format to a solitary focus on the thought of the sound. Once the mantra itself is transcended, the practitioner may have the experience of what the Maharishi calls the "source of the thought" or transcendental being. The TM state produces a marked effect on the physiological condition including respiration, heart rate, blood flow, EEG and basal skin resistance.

Wai qi. The transference of qi from the master to an individual person or object.

Western biofeedback therapy. Biofeedback is an alternative to drugs for the treatment of stress-induced pain such as migraines, hypertension and muscle spasms. Trained clinicians use biofeedback machines to gauge a person's internal bodily functions, to encourage the patient to focus on the activity inside the body and learn to identify the triggers which cause their symptoms. Patients are taught various forms of relaxation exercise, such as meditation, visualization and deep breathing, to relieve the symptoms, and may ultimately gain control over the systems. This is a prime example of the mind-body connection.

Yin and yang. A philosophy based on opposite principles, yin and yang. The two poles are complementary and both contain aspects of the other – nothing is absolutely yin or yang. The aspects constantly shift and interact until they manifest a relative balance suitable for the individual. *See also* **Yin qi and yang qi**.

Yin tang. The third eye point, also known as the upper dantian.

Ying qi and yang qi. In traditional Chinese medicine the theory exists that everything is in a constant state of transformation, where the goal is to maintain balance. Yin and yang are opposing forces, similar to day and night, black and white. Although the forces are opposing, they are interdependent – one does not exist without the other. Qi is energy in different states, moving in different directions. When not in balance, it can affect the state of health within an organism. Yin qi is the physical body or anatomy, and yang qi moves, disperses, descends and rises as the physiology of the organism. If qi is not moving (yang), it generally causes pain in the body (i.e. the yin). The theory of yin and yang can explain numerous functions of the body. For example, too much movement or work (yang) and not enough rest (yin) can manifest as nervousness and sleep deprivation in the body.

Yoga. Yoga is a physical exercise and a lifestyle practice. By holding a precise alignment of poses, it is possible to train your body, mind and breath, as well as making connection with your spirituality. Physically, yoga can improve flexibility, strength, balance and stamina. The psychological benefits include the reduction of anxiety and stress, and the subsequent improvement of mental clarity and sleep.

References

Adachi, Y., Aoki, T., Yoshihuku, Y., Yoshida, K. and Suzuki, S. (1998) "Study on the influence of emission from a 80KHz Quartz resonance system on the human body – NMR Analysis of Water." *Journal of International Society of Life Information Science 16*, 1, 60–66.

Adler, A. (1907) *Study of Organ Inferiority and Its Psychical Compensations.* New York: Mental and Nervous Diseases Publications Co.

Agishi, T. (1996) "Evaluation of Therapeutic External Qigong from the Viewpoint of the Western Medicine." *Journal of International Society of Life Information Science 14*, 1, 102–106.

Aldridge, D. (1993) "Is There Evidence for Spiritual Healing?" *Advances 9*, 4, 4–21.

American Psychiatric Association (1980) *Diagnostic and Statistical Manual of Disorders,* 3rd edn. Washington, DC: APA.

American Psychiatric Association (1994) *Diagnostic and Statistical Manual of Mental Disorders,* 4th edn. Washington, DC: APA.

Ansbacher, H.L. and Ansbacher, R.R. (1956) *The Individual Psychology of Alfred Adler.* New York: Harper and Row.

Arntz, W., Chasse, B. and Vincente, M. (2005) *What the Bleep Do We Know!?* Deerfield Beach, FL: Health Communications.

Badalamenti, A.F. (1985) "Energy and Psychical Pain." *Journal of Religion and Health 24*, 4, 316–342.

Bailey, L. (1990) "The Danger of Arousing Kundalini." In J. White (ed.) *Kundalini: Evolution and Enlightenment.* New York: Paragon House.

Barkley, R.A. (1988) "Attention Deficit Disorder with Hyperactivity." In E.J. Mash and L.G. Terdal (eds) *Behavioral Assessment of Childhood Disorders,* 2nd edn. New York: Guilford.

Barnes, L. (1998) "The Psychologizing of Chinese Healing Practices in the United States." In B.J. Good and M.J. Delvecchio Good (eds) *Culture, Medicine and Psychiatry 22*, 1. Amsterdam: Kluwer Academic.

Bassman, L. (1997) "Holistic Mental Health Care: Alternatives and Adjuncts to Psychotherapy and Medication." *The Humanistic Psychologist 25*, 138–149.

Baum, B. (1997) *The Healing Dimensions*. Tucson, AZ: Healing Dimensions, A.C.C. and West Press.

Beck, A., Rush, A., Shaw, B. and Emergy, G. (1979) *Cognitive Therapy of Depression*. New York: Guilford.

Becker, R.O. (1990) *Crosscurrents: The Promise of Electromedicine; the Perils of Electropolution*. New York: Tarcher/Penguin Putnam.

Benor, D. (1997) "Healing Research." *Advances 13*, 4, 75.

Benson, H. (1975) *The Relaxation Response*. New York: William Morrow.

Bergsman, O. and Wooley-Hart, L.A. (1973) "Differences in Electrical Skin Conductivity between Acupuncture Points and Adjacent Skin Areas." *American Journal of Acupuncture 1*, 27–32.

Brennan, B. (1988) *Hands of Light: A Guide to Healing through the Human Energy Field*. Toronto: Bantam.

Brown, C.C., Fischer, R., Wagman, A., Horrom, N. and Marks, P. (1977) "The EEG in Meditation and Therapeutic Touch Healing." *Journal of Altered States of Consciousness 3*, 2, 169–181.

Cao, Z., Zhao, L. and Zhang, L. (1989) "Functional Changes during the Process of Entering Qigong Quiescence." Second International Conference on Qigong, p.39.

Carnie, L.V. (2000) *Chi-Gung*. Minnesota, MN: Llewellyn.

Chan, I.W. (1987) "Introducing the Chinese Xexiangzhuang (Flying Crane) Qigong Therapy." *International Journal of Psychosomatics 34*, 4, 28–34.

Cleary, T. (1998) *The Essential Tao Translated*. Edison, NJ: Castle Books.

Cohen, K. (1997) *The Way of Qigong*. New York: Ballantine.

Cronkite, R. and Moos, R. (1995) "Life Contest, Coping Processes and Depression." In L.E. Beckham and W. Leber (eds) *Handbook of Depression*. New York: Guilford.

Cui, H.M. (1988) "Meridian System: Specialized Embryonic Epithelial Conduction System." *Shanghai Journal of Acupuncture 3*, 44–45.

Cunningham, O. (1981) "The Relationship of Psychic Healing and Insight-Oriented Treatment within an Expressive Framework." *Pratt Institute Creative Arts Therapy Review 2*, 15–25.

Davidson, J. (1987) *Subtle Energy*. Saffron Walden, UK: C.W. Daniel.

De Moor, M., Boomsma, D., Stubbe, J., Willemsen, G. and de Geus, E.J. (2008) "Testing Causality in the Association between Regular Exercise and Symptoms of Anxiety and Depression." *Archives of General Psychiatry 65*, 8, 897–905.

Depression Guideline Panel (1993) *Clinical Practice Guideline No. 5: Depression in Primary Care*. Volume 2: *Treatment of Major Depression*. Rockville, MD: US Department of Health and Human Services, Agency for Health Care Policy and Research, AHCPR Publication 93-0550.

Dockstader, L.S. and Barrett, S. (1998) "Stress Management through an Integrative Program of Qigong and Psychoneuroimmunology (PNI)." Second World Congress of Qigong, p.36.

Dou, L. and Zhang, Y. (1989) "The Observation of Qigong Effect on Brain Blood Supply." Second International Conference on Qigong, p.102.

Du, L. (1988) "Effect of Mind-Control in Qigong Exercises Investigated by an Infrared Thermovision Imager." First World Conference of Academic Exchange on Medical Qigong, p.183.

Dusek, J.A., Hasan, H.O., Wohlhueter, A.L., Bhasin, M. *et al.* (2008) "Genomic Counter-Stress Changes Induced by the Relaxation Response." PLoS One 3(7) e2576 doi:10.1371/journal.pone0002576.

Eisenberg, D.M., Davis, R.B., Ettner, S.L., Appel, S. *et al.* (1998) "Trends in Alternative Medicine Use in the United States 1990–1997." *Journal of the American Medical Association 280*, 1569–1575.

Epstein, M. (1995) *Thoughts Without a Thinker: Psychotherapy from a Buddhist Perspective.* New York: HarperCollins.

Eserick, J.W. (1987) *The Origins of the Boxer Uprising.* Berkeley, CA: University of California Press.

Fan, J.Y. (1990) "The Role of Gap Junctions in Determining Skin Conductance and Their Possible Relationship to Acupuncture Points and Meridians." *American Journal of Acupuncture 18*, 163–170.

Feng, L., Qian, J. and Peng, L. (1998) "The Influence of Qigong on DNA Mass." Fourth World Conference of Academic Exchange of Medical Qigong, pp.112–113.

Fromm, H.G., Carlson, P., Luckenbaugh, D., Waldeck, T. *et al.* (May, 2008) "Neural Response to Catecholamine Depletion in Unmedicated Subjects with Major Depressive Disorder in Remission and Healthy Subjects." *Archives of General Psychiatry 65*, 5, 521–531.

Gaik, F. (2003) "Merging East and West: A Preliminary Study Applying Qigong to Depresion as an Alternative and Complementary Treatment." Dissertation.

Gallo, F.P. (ed.) (2002) *Energy Psychology in Psychotherapy.* New York: W.W. Norton.

Guan, P. (1989) "Qigong and Human Body Science – The Relationship among Qigong, Human Blood and Development of Intelligence." Second International Conference on Qigong, p.54.

Guo, L. (1993) "Study of Application of Computer to Qigong Energy." Second World Conference of Academic Exchange for Medical Qigong, p.121.

Han, J. (1986) "Electroacupuncture: An Alternative to Antidepressants for Treating Affective Diseases?" *International Journal of Neuroscience 29*, 79–92.

Harris, L:B. (1994) "Kundalini and Healing in the West." *Journal of Near Death Studies 13*, 2, 75–79.

He, M.T. (1996) "Qigong Craze." *Psychology and Health 12*, 33.

He, Q., Zhang, J. and Li, J. (1988) "Effect of Different Qigong Exercises on EEG Manifested by Computer Analysis." First World Conference of Academic Exchange of Medical Qigong, p.37.

Hearne, K.M. (1982) "Energy Flow between Healer and Patient." *Journal of the Society for Psychical Research 51,* 792, 382–384.

Higuchi, Y., Kotani, Y., Higuchi, H. and Minegishi, Y. (1996) "Endocrine and Immune Response during Qigong Meditation." *Journal of International Society of Life Information Science 14,* 2, 278–279.

Higuchi, Y., Kotani, Y., Higuchi, H., Minegishi, Y. *et al.* (1997) "Endocrine and Immune Changes during Guolin New Qigong." *Journal of International Society of Life Information Science 15,* 2, 320–329.

Hills, C. (1990) "Is Kundalini Real?" In J. White (ed.) *Kundalini: Evolution and Enlightenment.* New York: Paragon House.

Hole, L.C. and Estes, R. (1998) "IBVA Interactive Brain Wave Analysis." Second World Congress of Qigong, p.40.

Hu, B. (1990) "Curative Effects of Qigong Movements." First International Congress of Qigong, p.102.

Huang, C. (1998) "Effective Energy Accumulation in the Human Body." Fourth World Conference of Academic Exchange of Medical Qigong, pp.191–192.

Huang, L. and Guan, H. (1989) The Change of Color and Temperature of Palm in State of Qigong." Second International Conference on Qigong, p.531.

Huang, Y. and Huang, Z. (1989) "Programs to Reform Conventional Teaching by Applying Qigong and Psychological Training." Second International Conference on Qigong, p.161.

Hutton, D., Liebling, D. and Leire, L. (1996) "Alternative Relaxation Training for Combat PTSD Veterans." Third World Conference of Academic Exchange for Medical Qigong, p.149.

Itoh, M., Miyazaki, H. and Takahashi, Y. (1996) "Imaging of Mind Using Positron Emission Topography." *Journal of International Society of Life Information Science 14,* 1, 76–80.

Jiang, L. and Tao, C. (1989) "Effect of Qigong on the Glucocorticoid Receptors of Human Peripheral Blood Lymphocytes and the Concentration of Cortisol." Second International Conference on Qigong, p.56.

Johnson, A.J. (2000) *Chinese Medical Qigong Therapy: A Comprehensive Clinical Text.* Pacific Grove, CA: International Institute of Medical Qigong.

Judith, A. (1996) *Eastern Body, Western Mind.* Berkeley, CA: Celestial Arts.

Kataoka, T., Sugiyama, N. and Matsumoto, M. (1997) "Effects of Qigong in Relation to the Capacity for Cancer Cell Disorder." *Journal of International Society of Life Information Science 15,* 2, 458–463.

Kawano, K. (1993) "Qigong's Suggestive Effect Seen in EEG." Second World Conference of Academic Exchange for Medical Qigong, p.991.

Kawano, K. (1998a) "EEG Changes with Progression of Qigong Practice." *Journal of International Society of Life Information Science 16*, 1, 148–153.

Kawano, K. (1998b) "Characterization of the EEG in Qigong and Hypnosis." *Journal of International Society of Life Information Science 16*, 2, 218–224.

Kawano, K., Shi, J.M. and Duan, L.Y. (1996) "The Frequency Change in Alpha Waves and the Appearance of Theta Waves during Qigong and Meditation." *Journal of International Society of Life Information Science 14*, 1, 22–31.

Kawano, K., Yamamoto, M., Kokubo, H., Sakaida, H. *et al.* (1997) "Difference in EEG in Methods of Qigong Practice and in Length of the Training Period." *Journal of International Society of Life Information Science 15*, 2, 365–367.

Kido, M. (1997) "Application of a Single Square Voltage Pulse Method." *Journal of International Society of Life Information Science 15*, 1, 60–70.

Kleinman, A. (1980) *Patients and Healers in the Context of Culture.* Berkeley, CA: University of California Press.

Kleinman, A. (1986) *Social Origins of Distress and Disease.* New Haven, CT: Yale University Press.

Kokubo, H., Yamamoto, M., Hirasawa, M., Sakaida, H. *et al.* (1998) "Development of Measuring System for nT-Order Magnetic Field Caused by Human Hands." *Journal of International Society of Life Information Science 16*, 1, 134–140.

Kreiger, D. (1990) "Two Decades of Research, Teaching and Clinical Practice." *Imprint 37*, 3, 83–88.

Kuhn, T.S. (1970) *The Structure of Scientific Revolutions*, 2nd edn. Chicago, IL: University of Chicago Press.

Larson, D., Wood, G. and Larson, S. (1993) "A Paradigm Shift in Medicine toward Spirituality?" *Advances 9*, 4, 39–49.

Lee, R.H. (1993) "Kirlian Imaging-Visual Investigations into the Nature and the Effects of Qigong." Second World Conference for the Academic Exchange of Medical Qigong, p.76.

Levin, J.S. and Coreil, J. (1986) "New Age Healing in the United States." *Social Science Medicine 23*, 9, 889–897.

Li, M., Chen, K. and Mo, Z. (1999) "Qigong Treatment for Drug Addiction." Third World Congress on Qigong.

Lim, J. (1988) "Qigong in Australia: An Effective Weapon against Stress." First World Conference of Academic Exchange of Medical Qigong, p.155.

Lin, C. (2000) *Spring Forest Qigong: Level I for Health.* Mennetonka, MN: Learning Strategies Corporation.

Linehan, M.M. (1993) *Cognitive Behavioral Treatment of Borderline Personality Disorder.* New York: Guilford.

Linehan, M.M., Tutek, D.A., Heard, H.L. and Armstrong, H.E. (1994) "Interpersonal Outcome of Cognitive Behavioral Treatment for Chronically Suicidal Borderline Patients." *American Journal of Psychiatry 151*, 1771–1776.

Lionberger, H.J. (1985) "An Interpretive Study of Nurses' Practice of Therapeutic Touch." Unpublished Doctoral Dissertation, University of California at San Francisco, Microfilm 382.

Liu, A., Zhao, J., Shong, C. and Wang, X. (1989) "Modified Actions of Qigong on Rat Axonal Sodium Channels." Second International Conference on Qigong, p.26.

Liu, A., Zhao, Y. and Du, Z. (1993) "Modified Effect of Emitted Qi on Close-Open Kinetic Process of Sodium Channels of Rat Cultural Neuron Cell." Second World Conference of Academic Exchange for Medical Qigong, p.98.

Liu, B., Jiao, J. and Li, Y. (1990) "Effect of Qigong Exercise on the Blood Level of Monamine Neurotransmitters in Patients with Chronic Diseases." *Chung His Chieh Ho Tsa Chih 10*, 4, 203–205. [Abstract] Qigong Institute Disc, Record 8910.

Liu, B., Jiao, K., Chne, Q., Li, Y. and Shang, L. (1988) "Effect of Qigong Exercise on the Content of Monamine Neurotransmitters in Blood." First World Conference of Academic Exchange of Medical Qigong, p.67.

Lu, Z., Wang, Y. and Yan, X. (1988) "A Method of Qi Field Detection." First World Conference of Academic Exchange for Medical Qigong, p.161.

Ma, J. (1988) "Mechanism of Qigong Magnetic Resonance." First World Conference of Academic Exchange for Medical Qigong, p.200.

Machi, Y. and Chu, W. (1996) "Physiological Measurement for Qigong Anesthesia." *Journal of International Society of Life Information Science 14*, 2, 129–152.

Machi, Y. and Liu, C. (1999) "Measurements of Physiological Effects of Internal Qigong: The Six-Word Practice (Rokujiketsu)." *Journal of International Society of Life Information Science 17*, 1, 32–53.

Machi, Y. and Zhong, C. (1996) "Physiological Measurements under Qigong Anesthesia." *Journal of International Society of Life Information Science 14*, 1, 63–75.

Marin, G. (1999) *Healing From Within with Chi Nei Tsang*. Berkley, CA: North Atlantic Books.

Mashansky, V.F. and Markov, U.V. *et al.* (1983) "Topography of the Gap Junctions in the Human Skin and Their Possible Role in the Non-Neural Sign Transduction." *Archives of Anatomical Histology and Embryology 84*, 53–60.

Mayer, M. (1998) "Psychotherapy and Qigong: Partners in Healing Anxiety." Second World Congress of Qigong, p.45.

McKnew, D.H., Jr., Cytryn, L. and Yahrals, H. (1983) *Why Isn't Johnny Crying?* New York: W.W. Norton.

Minegishi, Y., Watanabe, T., Kobabyashi, T., Yamaguchi, S. and Higuchi, Y. (1998) "Influences of Wujijinggong on Blood Serotonin and B-Endorphin Concentrations." *Journal of International Society of Life Information Science 16*, 1, 42–45.

Mojtabai, R. (2008) "National Trends in Psychotherapy by Office-Based Psychiatrists." *Archives of General Psychiatry 65*, 8, 962–970.

Moss, T. (1979) *The Body Electric.* New York: Jeremy P. Tarcher Inc.

Motoyama, H. (1978) *Science and the Evolution of Consciousness.* Brookline, MA: Autumn Press.

Myss, L.C. (1996) *Anatomy of the Spirit.* New York: Random House.

Needham, J. (1975) *Science and Civilization in China,* Volume 2. Cambridge: Cambridge University Press.

Ng, B. (1999) "Qigong Induced Mental Disorders: A Review." *Australian and New Zealand Journal of Psychiatry 33,* 197–206.

Nichols, C.R., Timmerman, R., Foster, R.S., Roth, B.J. and Einhorn, L.H. (1997) "Neoplasms of the Testes." In J.F. Holland, R.C. Baset, Jr., D.L. Morton, L.E. Frei *et al.* (eds) *Cancer Medicine,* 4th edn. Baltimore, MD: Williams and Wilkins.

Nishimoto, S. (1996) "Report on Autonomic Nervous System Changes and Pain Reduction Evinced by Patients Administered External Ki Therapy with Alpha Wave 1/f Music." *Journal of International Society of Life Information Science 14,* 2, 259–265.

Ogawa, T., Hayashi, L.S., Shinoda, N. and Ohnishi, N. (1988) "Changes of Skin Temperature during Emission of Qi." First World Conference of Academic Exchange for Medical Qigong, p.80.

Omura, Y. (1990) "Storing of Qigong Energy in Various Materials and Drugs (Qigongization): Its Clinical Application for Treatment of Pain, Circulatory Disturbance, Bacterial or Viral Infections, Heavy Metal Deposits and Related Intractable Medical Problems by Selectively Enhancing Circulation and Drug Uptakes." *Acupuncture Electrotherapeutics Research International Journal 15,* 137–157.

Page, C. (2000) *Frontiers of Health: From Healing to Wholeness.* Saffron Walden, UK: C.W. Daniel.

Pavek, R.R. (1988) "Effects of Qigong on Psychosomatic and Other Emotionally-Rooted Disorders." First World Conference of Academic Exchange for Medical Qigong, p.150.

Peng, X. and Liu, G. (1988) "Effect of Emitted Qi and Infrasonic Sound on Somatosensory Evoked Potential (SEP) and Slow Vertex Response (SVR)." First World Conference of Academic Exchange for Medical Qigong, p.331.

Pert, C. (1999) *Molecules of Emotion.* New York: Touchstone.

Post, A. and Cavaliere, S. (2003) *Unwinding the Belly.* Berkeley, CA: North Atlantic.

Prioreschi, P. (1995) *A History of Medicine.* Omaha, NE: Horatio Press.

Qigong Institute (1995) *Guidelines for Selecting Qigong Healers in the Scientific Research of Qigong.* Berkeley, CA: Qigong Institute Disc.

Qin, C., Yiang, J., Dong, E., Yang, I. *et al.* (1989) "Curative Effect of Qigong Therapy for Students with Neurasthenia." Second International Conference on Qigong, p.190.

Rao, K. (1991) "Healing Meditation and Anomalous Mental Phenomena." *Journal of Indian Psychology 9*, 1 and 2, 1–13.

Reid, D. (1998) *A Complete Guide to Chi-Gung.* Boston, MA: Shambhala.

Reuther, I. and Aldridge, D. (1998) "Treatment of Bronchial Asthma with Qigong Yang Sheng: A Pilot Study." *Journal of Alternative and Complementary Medicine 4*, 173–183.

Sakaida, H., Kokubo, H., Yamamoto, M., Hirasawa, M. and Kawano, K. (1998) "A Study with Various Simultaneous Measurements (VSM) on Physiological States Emitting Qi during Qigong." *Journal of International Society of Life Information Science 16*, 1, 29–41.

Sancier, K. (1990) "Healing with Qigong: Case Studies and Experimental Measurements by Muscle Testing." First International Congress of Qigong, p.110.

Sancier, K. (1996) "Anti-Aging Benefits of Qigong." *Journal of International Society of Life Information Science 14*, 1, 12–21.

Sancier, K. (1999) "Therapeutic Benefits of Qigong Exercises in Combination with Drugs." *Journal of Alternative and Complementary Medicine 5*, 4, 383–389.

Schwarz, J. (1980) *Human Energy Systems.* New York: Dutton.

Seyle, H. (1956) *The Stress of Life.* New York: McGraw-Hill.

Shan, H., Yan, H., Sheng, H. and Hu, S. (1989) "A Preliminary Evaluation on Chinese Qigong Treatment of Anxiety." Second International Conference on Qigong, p.165.

Shen, G. (1986) "Study of Mind-Body Effects and Qigong in China." *Advances 3*, 4, 134–142.

Shen, Z., Tone, L. and Lasayama, M. (1999) "Physiological Changes Caused by Wai Qi Fa Gong." *Journal of International Society of Life Information Science 17*, 1, 90–100.

Shibata, T. and Furiya, K. (1993) "Double-Blind Tests of Qi Transmission from Qigong Masters to Untrained Volunteers: Measurement of Qigong by Blood Analysis." *Japanese Mind-Body Science 2*, 1, 125–128.

Shigemi, K.S. (1994) "Storage and Circulation of Qi in Matter." *Chinese Journal of Somatic Science 4*, 1, 9. [Abstract] Qigong Institute Disc, Record 10860.

Sim, M.K. and Grewal, J. (1989) "Chinese Diaphragmatic Breathing as an Adjunct to Relaxation: Effects on EEG." *Medical Psychotherapy 2*, 157–162.

Stone, B. (1997) "Cultivating Qi." *Newsweek 130*, 4, 71.

Tang, C. and Sun, L. (1989) "Effects on Qigong on Excretion of Urinary Catecholamines." Second World Conference on Qigong, p.30.

Tang, C. and Wei, X. (1993) "Effect of Qigong on Personality." Second World Conference of Academic Exchange for Medical Qigong, p.921.

Tang, Y., Sun, C., Hong, Q., Liu, C. and Li, L. (1993) "Protective Effect of Emitted Qi on the Primary Culture of Neurocytes In Vitro Against Free Radical Damage." Second World Conference of Academic Exchange for Medical Qigong, p.100.

Thase, M. and Glick, I. (1995) "Combined Treatment." In I. Glick (ed.) *Treating Depression.* San Francisco, CA: Jossey Bass.

Tong, S. and Xe, P. (1990) "Qigong for Increasing Learning Ability." First International Congress of Qigong, p.124.

Tse, M. (1995) *The Root of Chinese Chi Kung.* Jamaica Plain, MA: Yang's Martial Arts Association.

Tsuda, Y., Sugano, H. and Shirouzu, S. (1999) "Does Suggestion Change the Effects of Qigong?" *Journal of International Society of Life Information Science 17,* 2, 284–286.

Uchida, L.S., Kuramoto, I. and Sugano, H. (1996) "Studies of Healing Effects Using the Kirlian Photography." *Journal of International Society of Life Information Science 14,* 2, 153–157.

Ueda, Y., Kashiba, H., Ishii, M. and Nakayoshi, T. (1997) "Physiological Measurement and Chaos Analysis for Qigong Practice and Acupuncture Treatment." *Journal of International Society Life Information Science 15,* 2, 306–319.

Wang, J. (1988) "Psychological Effects of Qigong." First World Conference of Academic Exchange for Medical Qigong, p.17.

Wang, J. (1993) "Role of Qigong on Mental Health." Second World Conference of Academic Exchange for Medical Qigong, p.93.

Wang, Z., Huang, J. and Wu, Z. (1988) "Preliminary Study of the Relationship between Qigong and Energy Metabolism: The Changes in Blood ATP Content." First World Conference of Academic Exchange for Medical Qigong, p.58.

Weil, A. (1995) *Spontaneous Healing.* New York: Random House.

West, M. (1979) "Meditation." *British Journal of Psychiatry 135,* 5, 457–467.

Westland, G. (1993) "Massage as a Therapeutic Tool." *British Journal of Occupational Therapy 56,* 4, 129–134.

Wilber, K. (1990) "Are the Chakras Real?" In J. White (ed.) *Kundalini: Evolution and Enlightenment.* New York: Paragon House.

Wildish, P. (2000) *The Book of Chi: Harnessing the Healing Force of Energy.* North Clarendon, VT: Tuttle.

Wirth, D.P. and Cram, J.C. (1993) "Multi-Site Electromyographic Analysis of Non-Contact Therapeutic Touch." *International Journal of Psychosomatics 40,* 1–4, 47–54.

Wood, C. (1985) "Reports on Mind-Body Research in Other Countries." *Advances 2,* 4, 67–73.

Wu, C. and Xu, P. (1988) "Spontaneous Dynamic Qigong, Involuntary Motion Qigong, and Psychological Medicine." First World Conference of Academic Exchange of Medical Qigong, p.123.

Wu, C.Y. (1992) "A Clinical Analysis of 76 Cases of Qigong-Induced Psychotic Disorders." *Journal of Clinical Psychological Medicine 2,* 7–9.

Xia, S.J. and Lin, Y.G. (1996) "Personality Profiles and EEG Characteristics of Patients with Qigong Deviations." *Chinese Qigong 2*, 17–19.

Xu, S. (1994) "Psychophysiological Reaction Associated with Qigong Therapy." *American Journal of Chinese Medicine 107*, 3, 230–233.

Yang, X., Liu, X. and Jia, Y. (1994) "Clinical Observation on Needling Extrachannel Points in Treating Mental Depression." *Journal of Traditional Chinese Medicine 14*, 14.

Yeh, T. (1990) "Mind, Body and Beyond: A Hypothesis on the Mechanism of Qi – The Resonance of the Human Body." International Congress of Qigong, p.117.

Yu, X., Xu, J., Shao, D., Wang, Y., Shang, J. and Lin, Y. (1998) "The Auxiliary Qigong Therapy for Parkinson's Disease and its Effects on EEG and P300." *Journal of International Society of Life Information Science 16*, 1, 73–82.

Zhang, T.L. and Xu, H.T. (1997) *Correcting Deviations from the Path of Qigong.* Beijing: House of People's Health.

Zheng, J.Y., Fan, J.Y., Zhang, Y.J., Guo, Y. and Xu, T.P. (1996) "Further Evidence for the Role of Gap Junctions in Acupoint Information Transfer." *American Journal of Acupuncture 24*, 291–296.

Zohar, D. (1990) *The Quantum Self.* New York: William Morrow.

SUBJECT INDEX

Author Index